SOMEHOW

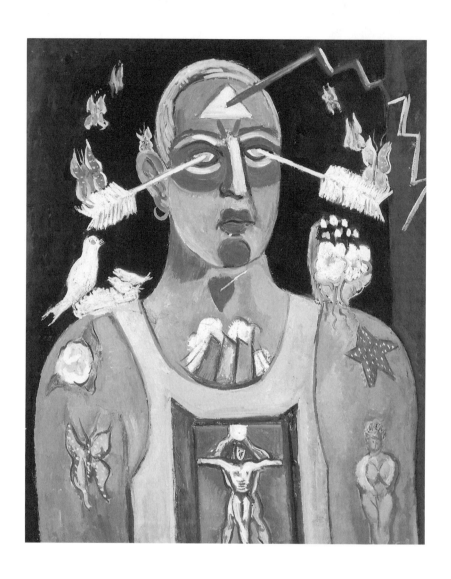

Hartley, *The Sustained Comedy (Portrait of an Object)*,
1939, oil on board, 28 1/8 × 22″, Carnegie
Museum of Art, Pittsburgh, Pennsylvania, gift of
Mervin Jules in memory of Hudson Walker, 76.64.

S O M_A M_PE_AH_S O_T W

THE AUTOBIOGRAPHY OF
Marsden Hartley

Marsden Hartley

Edited, with an introduction by *Susan Elizabeth Ryan*

The MIT Press   Cambridge, Massachusetts   London, England

Introduction and notes ©1995 Susan Elizabeth Ryan

"Somehow a Past: Prologue to Imaginative Living," "Somehow a Past," and appendices © Yale University.
Quotes from letters of Alfred Stieglitz and Gertrude Stein, and from letters and essays of Marsden Hartley, including variant texts of "Somehow a Past," all reprinted with the permission of the Yale Collection of American Literature, Beinecke Rare Book and Manuscript Library, Yale University.

This book was set in Centaur and Joanna by Graphic Composition, Inc.
Printed on recycled paper and bound in the United States of America.

Library of Congress Cataloging-in-Publication Data

Hartley, Marsden, 1877–1943.
    Somehow a past : the autobiography of Marsden Hartley / edited, with an introduction by Susan Elizabeth Ryan.
        p.   cm.
    Includes bibliographical references.
    ISBN 0-262-08251-9 (hb : alk. paper)
    1. Hartley, Marsden, 1877–1943.   2. Painters—United States—Biography.   I. Ryan, Susan Elizabeth.   II. Title.
    ND237.H3435A2   1996
    759.13—dc20
    [B]   96-15526
                                                                          CIP

To the memory of my mother,
Iva Dorothy Titus Ryan

CONTENTS

ILLUSTRATIONS

ACKNOWLEDGMENTS

My debt of gratitude to the following people dates back a long way: George Hersey, Roger Conover, Edna Keyes, and Alma McArdle, all of whom provided inspiration as well as support. Thanks for assistance and contributions from my colleagues at Louisiana State University: Mark Zucker, Richard Cox, and James Olney. And thanks to Irene Nero, Erin Reid, and to the graduate students who took my "Art and Autobiography" seminar in the fall of 1994, who made me see things I might otherwise have overlooked.

I have consulted with many scholars and specialists along the way and I am grateful to them all. Among these, Sue Davidson Lowe patiently answered questions about Alfred Stieglitz's relationship with Hartley, and Gail Scott provided me with advice at the outset of this project. Thanks to Robert Indiana, whose enthusiasm for Hartley got me started on Hartley in the first place.

The task of my research was lightened by individuals at several institutions. The bulk of Hartley's letters and manuscripts were given to Beinecke Library, Yale University, by his niece Norma Berger. I am particularly indebted to Patricia Willis, Curator of the Yale Collection of American Literature at Beinecke, and Danielle McClellan, Public Services Assistant.

In 1951 Ms. Berger also passed on to Bates College the contents of Hartley's last studio in Corea, Maine, including in addition to drawings and photos, many personal items such as Hartley's jewelry, wallets, and his collection of mementos and souvenirs. At the Museum of Art, Olin Arts

Center, Bates College, I was kindly assisted by Genetta McLean, Curator, William Low, and Anthony Shostak; and at Bates's Ladd Library, by Mary Riley, Curator of Special Collections.

Much work was done during the summer of 1995 thanks to the excellent networking skills of the research librarians at Cary Memorial Library, Lexington, Massachusetts.

I am especially grateful for the help I received from Kathleen Caruso and Daniele Levine at The MIT Press.

Finally, thanks to Paul Charlo and to Leonardo.

INTRODUCTION
Marsden Hartley: Practicing the "Eyes" in Autobiography

A cook. A cook can see. Pointedly in uniform, exertion in a medium. A cook

can see.

—"M—N H—," FROM GERTRUDE STEIN, "IIIIIIIIII,"
Geography and Plays

Some years before his death in a remote corner of coastal Maine, the American painter Marsden Hartley wrote that trying to recall the profile of the past was like trying to paint the contours of a mountain. He matched the inner vision of memory with the outer vision of eyesight. Neither is a simple act of recording; both involve something more. Throughout his life as a painter, Hartley studied mountains firsthand on three continents, from Mt. Katahdin in Maine to Popocatépetl in Mexico; he even pursued Cézanne's Mont Sainte-Victoire in southern France. But often to capture a particular mountain, Hartley had to paint it from memory, as with his mountainous New Mexican landscapes: after a series done on site in 1918–19, he produced another set called *Recollections* done entirely without models, while living in Berlin. For Hartley, the form visually scrutinized and the imprint on the mind of the form once seen come together in an act that is partly sensory and mechanical, but that is equally intimate and emotive—a compound of viewer and viewed. This synthetic visual memory is exactly what he set out to explore, verbally, when he wrote his autobiography.

This volume is very unlike the excellent accountings of Hartley and his œuvre that have appeared over the last fifteen years.[1] The concern here is with Hartley's own words about his life. He was born in 1877 and died in 1943 and, though his work was never widely popular in his lifetime, he was recognized among an international coterie of artists and intellectuals as an idiosyncratic artist of visual strength and conceptual originality, and noted for his dogged pursuit of the meaning of artistic practice. Born to a poor immigrant family in Maine during the Victorian era, and traditionally trained at the Cleveland School of Art and at the Chase School and National Academy of Design in New York, Hartley was nevertheless temperamentaly drawn to experimentation over virtuousity, and lived at a time when he could seek out and engage with other creative individuals who were challenging the boundaries of genre and style, such as Alfred Stieglitz and Gertrude Stein. Hartley became a precocious interpreter of fauvism, cubism, and German expressionism, intuitively navigating the heady discourses of abstraction current in his day, and emerging with something, as Stein herself described his painting, that keeps "your attention freshened"—as exemplified by his famous series of symbolic "German Officer" portraits done on the eve of World War I in Berlin.[2] From that precocious body of postcubist painting, Hartley's art, rather than charting another art-historical "ism," evolved and changed in ways difficult to categorize, waxing between the poles of realism and nonrepresentationalism, and culminating in his forcefully architected, vividly chromatic paintings of figures and landscapes done in Maine at the end of his life. Never in any sense a settled individual, and always giving a solitary impression, Hartley beautifully typifies the art-historical archetype of the saturnine artist.[3] A "gnarled, New England spinsterman," as Mabel Dodge characterized him, Hartley was moody, gifted, homosexual but unable to form lasting intimacies with anyone, a wanderer, insistently empirical and probing, and always leveraged by a keen sense of his own flaws and deficiencies.[4] Hartley presents the contemporary scholar with an untidy field of inquiry, where it is virtually impossible to banish biography from any discussion of his art.

The situation is not made simpler by the fact that Hartley was both highly prolific as a painter and also voluminous as a writer and poet. During his life he produced a book of prose essays on art and literature, *Adventures in the Arts* (1921), and three volumes of poetry, *Twenty-Five Poems* (1923), *Androscoggin* (1940), and *Sea Burial* (1941), and contributed often to journals and magazines as wide ranging as *Camera Work, Dial, New Republic, Poetry, New York Dada, Art and Archeology,* and *Vanity Fair.*[5] But the published writings represent only a fraction of the vast number of unpublished essays and poems Hartley wrote over the course of his life, many of which he collected and prepared for publication, with titles like "The Spangle of Existence," "Varied Patterns," and "Elephants and Rhinestones" (prose) and "Bach for Breakfast," "Laughter of Steel," and "Patterns for Prayers," (poetry). A vast body of manuscript material, including all the autobio-

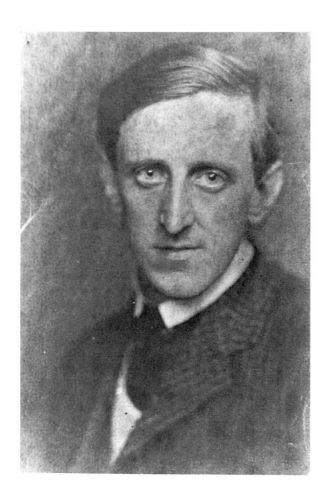

Marsden Hartley, 1908, by an unknown
photographer, Marsden Hartley Memorial
Collection, Museum of Art, Bates College.

graphical manuscripts, was deposited after Hartley's death in the Yale Collection of American Literature, Beinecke Rare Book and Research Library (hereafter YCAL), by Hartley's niece, Norma Gertrude Berger. What is represented here is Hartley's project to recover a verbal vision of his own past over a period of some eight to ten years at the end of his life, a project that resulted in a group of manuscripts all bearing the same strange title: "Somehow a Past."

One manuscript has been singled out for special treatment here. Entitled, like the others, "Somehow a Past" and subtitled "Prologue to Imaginative Living," it is the most complete essay in the group. Written in Hartley's hand, it is far from flawless and contains several discontinuities. Nevertheless it forms a coherent narrative that is datable, through internal references, to 1933.[6]

In comparison to "Somehow a Past: Prologue to Imaginative Living" (hereafter SAP1), two other versions of Hartley's autobiography make up the rest of the group in the YCAL. Hartley seems to have worked on these intermittently from 1937 through 1941 or 1942. They bear the same title but are subtitled, respectively, "A Sequence of Memories Not to Be Called an Autobiography" (hereafter SAP2) and "A Journal of Recollection" (hereafter SAP3). Both SAP2 and SAP3 are more fragmented and less comprehensive than SAP1. The former repeat, often in a diffuse or melodramatic way, much of the material in SAP1, but they also add accounts that SAP1 lacks. Accordingly, selected excerpts from SAP2 and SAP3 are included here as appendices.

Since the handwritten material as it exists today in the YCAL was not dated, documented, or organized by Hartley (as far as we know), some margin of error is inevitable in this arrangement, especially since narrative gaps and discontinuous paginations occur in all the manuscripts. There is no guarantee that no page or segment ever migrated from one version to another, especially between SAP1 and SAP2 (mix-ups involving SAP3 are less likely since its pages are on unique, three-hole-punched, lined paper and grouped in a series of ring binders). Throughout all the manuscripts, pen color, paper, and other physical details vary somewhat, but not in ways that can confirm any particular reorganization. However, for our purposes,

First page of manuscript, "Somehow a Past:
Prologue to Imaginative Living," Marsden Hartley
Collection, Yale Collection of American Literature,
Beinecke Rare Book and Manuscript Library,
Yale University.

the integrity of SAP I is based on both its internal references and its relative continuity. Its contents and form agree convincingly with the documented process of its writing, which took place within about three reclusive weeks when Hartley was otherwise occupied painting mountains in Bavaria.

Hartley also wrote two different autobiographical poems, both at the YCAL, and both also entitled "Somehow a Past." [7] Neither can be dated with accuracy. Thus printing one of the poems but not the other, here with the 1933 version of the prose autobiography, is unjustifiable in terms of evidence. But the poems are useful for succinctly identifying the sense of self revealed by Hartley's autobiographical voice. Each poem in its own way, and especially the one beginning, "Plain, simple, simple, plain . . ." that precedes SAP I here, discloses the vagrant, melancholic mood that pervades Hartley's personal narrative. Lines like "I saw it all through a groove in the sky" poeticize the autobiographer's characteristic distance or even absence from the action of his life. "Somehow a Past," after all, would seem an unlikely title for an autobiography. It is lukewarm and unenterprising, as if its author felt himself a passive figure, a spectator—the term Hartley used to describe himself in the later manuscripts. Yet "Somehow a Past," despite its unauthoritativeness, was the title he gave to the poems, and it was the title he remained committed to as he pursued his autobiographical rewriting up to the end of his life.

One other pertinent document that is illustrated rather than reprinted here is a typescript that seems to be by Hartley himself, and corrected in his own handwriting. It is a table of contents or list of text subheadings that closely coincides with the 1933 manuscript (SAP I), and may (or may not) be contemporary with it. The profile of episodes the list represents, and many of its individual headings, roughly match SAP I. However, the list also ends with entries covering Hartley's 1933 travels to Hamburg and finally Bavaria itself, plus perhaps two poetic segments that have been lost from SAP I, or were never written.

The Making of a Manuscript

Most Hartley scholars comment at some length on this artist's aesthetic bipartisanship. In his early years he based his creative endeavors on solitude

Somehow a Past.

Plain,simple--simple,plain.

I am an English Yankee.

Transferred to Ohio.

The Magic of New York.

I return to New England.

New York,and----### "291".

Then Paris.

27 rue de Fleurus.

Berlin--

New York again--1915.

Mabel and her Salon.

The big summer at Provincetown.

New Mexico,and the other West.   1916-1917.

Bermuda.   1918--1919.

The Auction of 1920--and Paris again.

Berlin,and the Inflation,and the news
of Alice Miriam's death.

Vienna--Florence--Rome--1923.

The south of France..1925.

Cezanne's Aix.   1926--1929.

The Return to New England.   1930.   Dogtown.

I get the Fellowship,and there is Mexico.

Mexico.   1932.   Hart Crane.

Northward Now.   1933.

Hamburg,and the third Reich.

Bavaria--Ludwig's Paradiso.

Draft table of contents for "Somehow a Past,"
Marsden Hartley Collection, Yale Collection of
American Literature, Beinecke Rare Book and
Manuscript Library, Yale University.

and spirituality, working "almost wholly from the imagination."[8] Later, he denounced that approach in favor of "life lived," and his conviction that the artist must remain fixed upon the objective world. For most of his career he vacillated between these poles. The Hartley who is roused by military spectacle in Berlin contrasts with the Hartley working alone in humble North Lovell, Maine, or in alpine Garmisch-Partenkirchen; and with the Hartley who was fascinated by alchemy and Paracelsus. Hartley's lifelong task of reconciling his outer and inner selves, his choice making between the factual and the mystical, generated a self-referential framework for nearly all his writings.[9] Naturally, Hartley's earliest artist's statements have a strong autobiographical flavor. In his 1914 catalog statement for his first exhibition at Alfred Stieglitz's avant-garde gallery, 291, he explains:

> It is the artist's business to select forms suitable to his own specialized experience . . . True modes of art are derived from modes of individuals understanding life. . . . The new wonder of the moment. The Creator never loses his sense of wonder . . . The present exhibition is the work of one who sees—who believes in what is seen—and to whom every picture is as a portrait of that something seen.[10]

Portraiture is a formative idea for Hartley, and applies not only to his approach to painting but also to his writing and, ultimately, to his autobiography. Indeed, within the cultural context surrounding Hartley's artistic development before and after World War I, portraiture was a signature genre, and the liberation of portraiture from its traditional focus on faces was the avant-garde practice par excellence in Paris and New York.[11] Marcel Duchamp, Francis Picabia, Marius de Zayas, and Charles Demuth were among those in Hartley's circle who assembled abstract and/or symbolic forms in works they called "portraits"; others, like Georgia O'Keeffe, imposed the portrait format on the inanimate world. Hartley called his first abstract paintings, done in Europe in 1912, "portraits of moments." But Hartley's particular concept of portraiture seems to have included the idea of personal memory. His well-known early German Officer portraits, the subjects of the 1914 exhibition, are symbolic concoctions that very much recall popular Victorian keepsakes of deceased loved ones. These were homely collages on velvet made of snapshots and bits of clothing and memorabilia pressed under glass—a person's portrait via his effects.[12] Throughout his career, Hartley's use of the term persisted and broadened, and ultimately referred to a mode of subjective perception. His "every picture as a portrait of something seen" impales objective reality on the vectors of visual contact.

In 1917 Hartley, perhaps partly in response to Gertrude Stein's abstract literary portraits that he probably read early in 1912, drafted some poems that have not survived of personal impressions that he called "portrait intimations."[13] In the ensuing years, as he began doing more writing, something of the same thinking may have stimulated his interest in autobiography. From the first, he seems to have viewed autobiography as something outwardly impersonal. He began a series of poems called "Laughter of Decision" in 1920, which he referred to as autobiography and in which, as he wrote Stieglitz, "I say very little about myself—excepting that what pours through me registers its own indelible fluid."[14]

Then in 1921 a quasi-autobiographical essay, "Concerning Fairy Tales and Me," appeared in a collection of Hartley's essays, *Adventures in the Arts.* This book was dedicated to Alfred Stieglitz and published by the Washington Square publisher Charles Boni. Like the 291 catalog essay, "Concerning Fairy Tales and Me" is an editorial on the subject of the imagination. Hartley links his taste for it to his lonely childhood but offers little biographical detail—it does not, for example, speak of his mother's early death.[15] However, Hartley's first real attempt at autobiography—a somewhat awkward and painful one—may have grown directly out of that essay and that book project. In 1923, when Hartley and Albert Boni, Charles's brother and associate, were both in Berlin, the latter developed several more publishing proposals for Hartley's writing and paintings, including a volume that would be part of a projected series on American artists, each a portfolio of prints and introductory information (which ultimately never came to pass).[16] Hartley had Stieglitz send him photographs of his works that had passed through 291, and when they arrived it probably gave Hartley his first overview of his own career.[17] Within a few

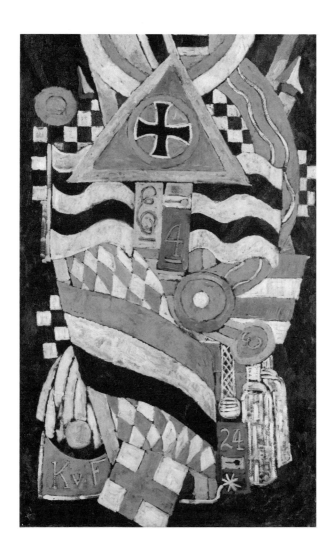

Hartley, *Portrait of a German Officer*, 1914, oil on
canvas, 68 1/4 × 41 3/8″, The Metropolitan
Museum of Art, New York, The Alfred Stieglitz
Collection, 1949, 49.70.42.

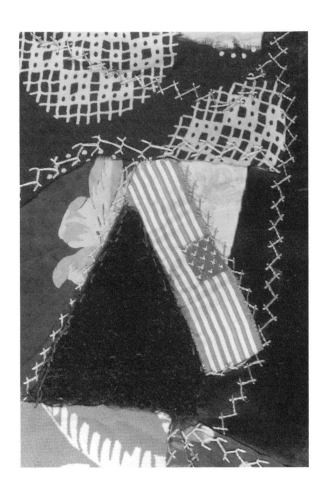

Keepsake quilt from Manchester, New Hampshire,
ca. 1900, detail, collection of the editor, photo by
Mark Kleiner. It is hand-stitched from pieces of
family members' clothes and hat ribbons.

months, he produced a four-page resume that presented its subject, somewhat naively, as a self-willed and self-sufficient native New England genius. The essay dealt freely with the facts, in particular rearranging the events of his early 291 connections, and barely mentioning Stieglitz. Hartley blithely forwarded the typescript to Stieglitz in October, which led to an angry reply from the latter correcting Hartley's account. "What an ass a man like Hartley is in spite of his talents," an injured Stieglitz wrote Rebecca Strand.[18] The result was a four-year-long rift during which Stieglitz barely showed Hartley's work.[19]

During that time Hartley was mostly in Europe—drifting psychologically, experimenting stylistically, and enduring physical and financial difficulties. By 1929 he was back in the United States and back in Stieglitz's (relative) good graces. Ideas about writing autobiography must have remained on his mind because it was during that year, working alone in the severe landscape of Dogtown in Gloucester, Massachusetts, that he seems to have acquired and read the archetypal autobiography of transformation, St. Augustine's *Confessions*.[20]

"Somehow a Past" (SAP1) followed shortly after. It was the longest piece of writing that he had ever undertaken, he reported, and it took place in November and December 1933, within a unique set of circumstances.[21] Hartley was alone in Bavaria, a sojourn that was itself a return and a kind of recollection, since he had more or less retraced the steps of his intense 1913 visit to the alpine home of German expressionist painter Franz Marc in nearby Sindelsdorf. This time Hartley stayed in Garmisch-Partenkirchen, in a modest *pensione*, the Haus Schober, living and working on a strict budget. It was a particularly concentrated period. He undertook a close study of what he referred to as mountain portraits—Alpspitze, Dreitorspitze, Waxenstein.[22] For support in this approach he drew upon qualities he identified in paintings in the Alte Pinakothek in Munich (which he visited in November), notably Leonardo da Vinci's *Madonna with a Carnation* (c. 1475) with its primeval mountain backdrop, and Albrecht Dürer's riveting, Christlike self-portrait of 1500. Of that, Hartley wrote,

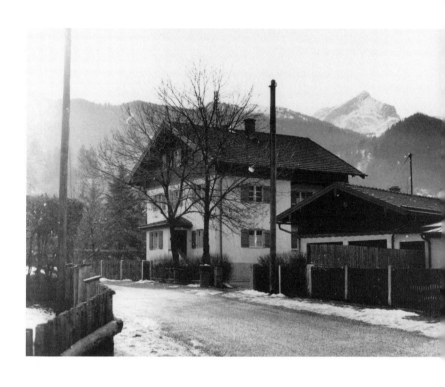

Haus Schober, Garmisch-Partenkirchen, Germany,
Elizabeth McCausland papers, Archives of
American Art, Smithsonian Institution.

It is all around the best portrait that has ever been done by anyone at any time ... Dürer seemed to have all that the eye can have, he saw things exactly as they were, and knew how to convey that impression ... I would like to make a painting of a mountain and have it have all that this portrait has.[23]

In the years 1929 through 1933 Hartley continued to read biography and autobiography, especially of the spiritual variety. He wrote to Rebecca Strand that he had read or reread the *Histoire d'une âme* of St. Thérèsa of Lisieux (1898), Cardinal Newman's *Apologia Pro Vita Sua* (1864), and Giovanni Papini's *Life of St. Augustine* (1930).[24] Later he wrote to Stieglitz of this time, saying that in the mountains he had undergone an epiphany that reminded him of Augustine, and which he described melodramatically:

The singular experience in the Alps—during a walk in the afternoon snow up the valley at Garmisch-Partenkirchen—seeing the keystone drop ... [the feeling was of a] conversion—or equal to what St. Augustine's follower called the "mystery of opening," and the whole vision of life was opened and I knew the work of my life had been completed.[25]

But every bit as important as these introspective encouragements was an autobiographical stimulus of a completely different nature: Gertrude Stein's newly published *Autobiography of Alice B. Toklas.* She, arguably after Stieglitz, was the second powerful mentor in Hartley's career. Hartley met Stein during his first trip to Europe in 1912. He records that he was brought to one of her famous Saturday evenings by someone named Carlock, and introduced as a friend of the painter Lee Simonson.[26] Afterward, Hartley visited Stein and her companion at 27 rue de Fleurus on Saturdays and at other, "nonofficial" times. Their growing respect and friendship, with Stein playing the role of guru, generated a correspondence that continued until just a few years before Hartley's death.[27] We learn from *The Autobiography of Alice B. Toklas* that Hartley read some of Stein's work in

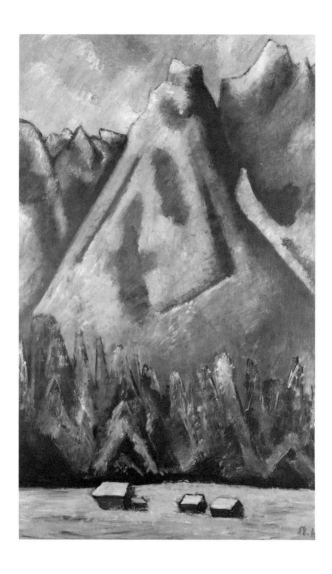

Hartley, *Waxenstein Peaks, Garmisch-Partenkirchen*, 1933,
oil on canvas, 32 × 20 1/2″, Yale University Art
Gallery, gift of Russell Lynes, B. A. 1932, in
memory of his brother, George Platt Lynes.

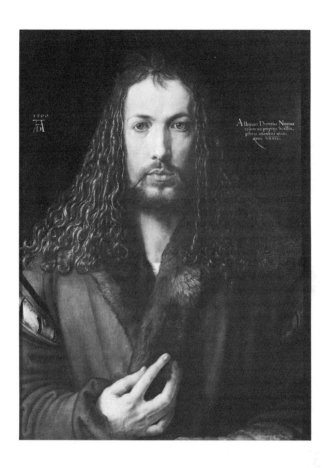

Albrecht Dürer, *Self-Portrait at Twenty-Eight Years Old
Wearing a Coat with Fur Collar,* 1500, Alte Pinakothek,
Munich, Germany (photo: Giraudon/Art Resource,
New York).

manuscript. By his own account in SAPI, Hartley's pictures prompted her remark, "at last, an original American." Hartley prided himself in her support and took it as validation for the circuitous paths he sometimes took in his career.

Hartley spent most of 1912 in Paris and then moved on to Berlin where he felt happier. Here he became ensconced in warm, familylike surroundings of his new friends, the German sculptor Arnold Rönnebeck, his fiancée Alice Miriam Pinch, and his cousin, Lieutenant Karl von Freyburg of the Prussian guard, all of whom he had met in Paris. He wrote to Stein:

> I do like Deutschland. I think I shall like it for long—I feel as if I were rid of the art monster of Paris and can sit down and be content with the tamer cubs. . . . But there are some features of Paris I do miss—I do miss 27.[28]

Hartley remained there, with one break spent back in America, until shortly after the outbreak of World War I. He had entrusted four paintings to Gertrude's care in Paris, and wrote to offer her one, which she said she could not accept but that she would buy a drawing. He told her not to send the money but hold onto it as a reserve in case of emergency—which came soon enough (a matter of weeks)—and upon Hartley's next injunction Stein forwarded forty dollars to Berlin by wire. Hartley worshipped Stein and Stein was able to write expansively on Hartley's behalf, as in a letter to Stieglitz:

> In his painting he has done what in Kandinsky is only a direction. Hartley has really done it. He has used color to express a picture and he has done it so completely that while there is nothing mystic or strange about his production it is genuinely transcendent. . . . There is another quality in his work that is very striking and that is the lack of fatigue or monotony that one gets in looking at his things. In some way he has managed to keep your attention freshened and as you look you keep on being freshened. There is not motion but there is an absence of the stillness that even in the big men often leads to non-existence.[29]

Around 1913 Stein included Hartley, identified as "M—N H—," as one of the characters in a dramatic dialogue entitled, "IIIIIIIII," a dialogue that shares an extreme of linguistic abstraction with the almost contemporary *Tender Buttons*, a collection of poetic pieces that are in a sense portraits of things. Stein mailed a copy of "IIIIIIIII" to Hartley in Germany, and he wrote back reacting to her unconventional characterization of him:

> It seems to have another kind of dynamic power—a kind of shoot to it and I feel my own color very much in what I say—my own substance. "Peaceable in the rest of the stretch" I say somewhere. It is so good for I feel that way.[30]

In return, in 1915 or 1916 he painted her symbolic portrait, entitled *One Portrait of One Woman*, with the central word, "MOI."[31] Above the word is a cup and saucer that signify Stein in many ways, but for Hartley must have recalled the tea he served the first time she and Alice came to his studio to see his paintings, an event recounted in SAP I.

More than a decade and a half later, at the age of fifty-six, living and painting in the Bavarian mountains, Hartley wrote again to Stein in Paris, exclaiming over what he had heard about her newest book, *The Autobiography of Alice B. Toklas* (published in 1933), and begging her to send him a copy (appendix I). Two weeks later he wrote another letter, thanking her with near hysterical enthusiasm, an extreme case of the fuss he always made over her kindness toward him. Her responses are lost, but Stein seems to have filled Hartley's request with a personally inscribed copy.

In his 1933 correspondence to Stein, capping the argument about how he deserved her book, Hartley named several quite different autobiographies he had read recently—popular ones by performers and adventurers such as the singers Emma Eames and Ernestine Schumann-Heink, the actor Otis Skinner, and the deep-sea diver Thomas Eadie.[32] These fast and easy moving tales supplied Hartley with model *vitae activae*, compared to Saint Augustine's *vita contemplativa*. They describe flamboyant lives and yet, like a latter-day Augustine, each author confesses how he or she found a

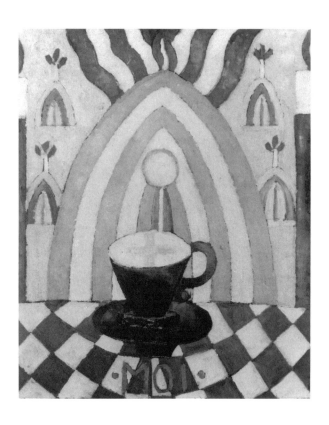

Hartley, *One Portrait of One Woman*, 1913–16, oil on
composition board, 32 × 21 3/8″, University of
Minnesota, Minneapolis, bequest of Hudson
Walker from the Ione and Hudson Walker
Collection, 78.21.64.

true path in life. Hartley must have suspected that such bell-curve narratives of self-definition would be utterly unlike Stein's simulation of life's immediacy, her accountings of undifferentiated streams of events in *The Autobiography of Alice B. Toklas.*

After finishing that book, in letters to his niece Norma Berger, Hartley divulged mild displeasure that it devoted only two lines to him (appendix 2). He also announced his decision to have, as he called it, a "Little Past" of his own. By December 5, he was reporting to Norma that the manuscript had reached the point where he had "just left Amsterdam and am on the way to Hamburg which was all last April" (appendix 2). But SAP1 ends in Amsterdam—literally in front of Rembrandt's *The Nightwatch,* and does not move on to Hamburg or Partenkirchen. Nor, for that matter, do either SAP2 or SAP3. Neither of these, in fact, takes his life story past his experiences in New York some twenty years earlier.

"Imaginative Living"

Hartley's conception of "Somehow a Past" was as a project, a kind of experiment, something spontaneous yet at the same time rooted in a fascination with autobiography that had been growing in him for some time. Bavaria offered him a sublime backdrop for meditation, and the time and isolation to proceed undistracted. He divided his days among writing (which probably took place in the morning), alpine trekking to sketch peaks in the afternoon, and reading and writing letters in the evening.[33] The latter reveal that his head was filled with ideas of portraiture and mountains, and with the recurrent problem of how to square truth to observed reality with truth of conception and character—the workings of objective and subjective perception. His ideas progressed further this time, in response to the Munich trips to view Dürer and Leonardo paintings. But the roots of his thinking went back to his earliest exposure to ideas concerning the self versus the world, Hartley's own first "conversion experience," his reading of Emerson.

Hartley noted in all versions of "Somehow a Past," and in countless other writings, that a key event of his youth was being given a copy of

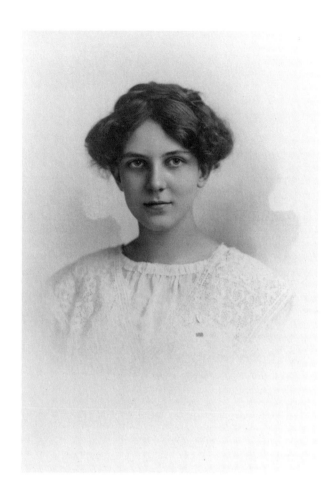

Norma Gertrude Berger (Hartley's niece), Marsden
Hartley Collection, Yale Collection of American
Literature, Beinecke Rare Book and Manuscript
Library, Yale University.

Emerson's *Essays* (1841) by Nina Waldeck, one of his earliest art teachers. According to one statement by Norma Berger, Waldeck also told Hartley he resembled Emerson, both physically and biographically.[34] In any event, Hartley carried the book around on his person, like a Bible, for years afterward.[35] Recent writers have pointed out the probable influence of Emerson's essay style on Hartley's, and that the transcendentalist's effect on Hartley as a writer was catalytic, since the youth had not finished high school and claimed "never to have read a book" until he encountered Emerson. Hartley's attraction for the balance of his adult life, to philosophical and mystical texts, suggests nothing short of an intellectual transformation. However, in SAPI, Hartley himself describes his childhood self as meditative. He was interested in the literary figures of Yorkshire, near his family's home, and was friends at school with avid students, future professors, and government leaders. All this is at odds with the notion that Waldeck and Emerson delivered Hartley from a life launched in ignorance.

Nevertheless, Emerson's writings must have given support to Hartley's struggle with descriptive/imaginative dichotomies in painting and perhaps also encouraged qualities in Hartley's expository style—its preaching tone and easy glide between crystalline fact and filmy abstraction. Yet, for all that Emerson stressed individual experience as the basis for comprehending the spirit, when Hartley treated big themes in his essays he seems always more pointedly self-referential. Any number of comparisons might be found between texts by Hartley and Emerson, but one example here will suffice. Here is Emerson, in his essay "Art" from *Essays:*

> Thus in our fine arts, not imitation, but creation is the aim. In landscapes, the painter should give the suggestion of a fairer creation than we know. The details, the prose of nature he should omit, and give us only the spirit and splendor. He should know that the landscape has beauty for his eye, because it expresses a thought which is to him good: and this, because the same power which sees through his eyes, is seen in that spectacle; . . . In a portrait, he must inscribe the character, and not the features, and must esteem the man who sits to him as himself only an imperfect picture or likeness of the aspiring original within.[36]

And also:

> The artist must employ symbols in use in his day and nation, to convey
> his enlarged sense to his fellow men.[37]

In "Dissertation on Modern Painting" (1921) Hartley writes:

> Art is the exact personal appreciation of a thing seen, heard, or felt in
> terms of itself.... To illustrate externals means nothing, because the
> camera is the supremely edifying master of that.... The thing must be
> brought clearly to the surface in terms of itself.... Symbolism can never
> quite be evaded in any work of art because every form and movement
> that we make symbolizes a condition in ourselves.[38]

But Hartley's autobiographical manuscript SAPI is very different. The
painter immersed himself in the rush of life, rather like Stein's *Autobiography
of Alice B. Toklas.* He makes present the past via memory, by living it over
again, creating a kind of chronicle in retrospect, rather than rendering a
unified reinterpretation. "I have never tried so long a piece of writing before," he wrote Norma, "and it has proven rather amusing to me to see
how much I could bring up in memory by living it over again." In the act
of writing, Hartley exchanges the measured life of St. Augustine for the
immediate one of Emerson and Gertrude Stein, so at least the first version
of "Somehow a Past" is redeemed from being a salvation saga or apologia
by the tumbling together of major and minor episodes, unsorted, one
after another.

Thus, the autobiographical precedent that bears most closely on
Hartley's SAPI is the one that stirred him into action, *The Autobiography of
Alice B. Toklas.* Hartley's writing even exhibits a smattering of the book's
chattiness and anecdotalism as well as its offhand, unceremonious flow of
events. Occasionally, in Hartley's manuscript, one finds passages that approach Steinese. For example, one of Stein's descriptions of Saturday evenings at the rue de Fleurus goes:

When we went into the atelier there was already quite a number of people in the room, scattered groups, single and couples all looking and looking. Gertrude Stein sat by the stove talking and listening and getting up to open the door and go up to various people talking and listening.[39]

And Hartley describes Stein's description:

It is without doubt the best portrait of a room that has been done by any of the moderns. It is a most speaking likeness. It is the room around Alice and Gertrude—it is them in the room it is the room with everybody passing through it and some of us remaining in it in whatever degree we could remain.

Only Hartley's autobiography is far simpler than the Stein-Toklas production. As opposed to the latter's externalized viewpoint that constructs a self always in the eyes of the other, Hartley's manuscript is clearly the voice of a man alone, talking to a reader who seems to be himself. He appears to have had no plan to publish it, either then, or several years later when he began revising it. He told his niece it was an "exercise in memory":

And when I get away from here it will be more difficult, so maybe I can get it done here. . . . It will interest someone to read it even if it is only you and maybe a dozen others I could think of.

The exercise was probably even therapeutic. The sojourn in Bavaria ended a difficult decade for Hartley, and marked the end of his life abroad as well.

At the onset of that decade, in 1920–21, he had become involved with New York Dada and even served as secretary of the Société Anonyme, though he abandoned that task dispiritedly. Intermittent periods of aimlessness and depression, which he had felt since his return from the productive years in Germany before the war, intensified. He was destitute. Dorothy Norman recorded that he outlined to Stieglitz a plan for a Dada suicide. He would go to Florence, "write a book of hate," send it to his friends, and kill himself.[40] Instead, thanks to Stieglitz's holding an auction of Hartley's works in 1921, he did go to Florence but did not die; and he wrote not a diatribe, but a constructive collection of criticism, *Adventures in the Arts.* He then spent the great part of 1924–28 traveling throughout Europe funded by a four-year stipend arranged by American diplomat William Bullitt and his associates for Hartley's support. In these years Hartley wrote introspective essays on the art he studied during his travels (which he compiled for an intended book called "Varied Patterns" that was never published[41]). His painting progressed from symbolic abstraction to a schematized representationalism, and finally to a Cézannesque perceptualism (painting Cézanne's very landscapes in southern France), that met with little approval among his supporters back home. He returned to America after the stock market crash of 1929, impoverished and ill with chronic bronchitis. He was thinking about death once again. In 1931, before leaving for Mexico on a Guggenheim grant, he even asked Norma to look into the costs of filing a will and arranging for his own cremation.[42]

Hartley traveled to Bavaria straight from Mexico on his own thin resources, rendered even thinner by the plummeting deutsche mark. Unlike his previous tours of the cities and southern resorts of Europe, where he routinely partook of the popular attractions, in Bavaria he had neither the funds nor the inclination for conviviality. But he emerged soothed from the autobiographical interlude and the epiphany in the lonely landscape. Hartley's odd subtitle for SAPI, "Prologue to Imaginative Living," suggests a beginning, not an ending, as if he believed his lifelong conflict between the spirit and the world was finally resolved in a renewed conviction of the unity between making art and living life.[43] He spent his last nine years (1934–43) in America, mostly in Maine and New York, engaged in one of the two most successful and prolific periods in his career as a painter—the other being the 1914–15 period in Germany.

We must assume that the autobiographical project demanded of Hartley an unusual level of concentration, since he could have had little documentary support. He was not a regular journalizer.[44] Instead of diaries Hartley wrote letters. He was an exhaustive correspondent—today there exist quantities of correspondence with Stieglitz and Berger as well as friends like Rebecca Strand, Adelaide Kuntz, and Isabel Duthet (Mme. Gaston Lachaise); Stein, of course; and many others. Whatever impulse he had to set down daily reactions to events, artistic ideas and plans, or emotional outpourings, he routinely did it in letters—the transient subgenre of autobiography—and sent them off without keeping copies. Of course, it is possible that Hartley had with him copies of the "Varied Patterns" travel essays, which would have functioned as notes. It is also possible that he had some other records, perhaps a travel diary, and that such items have disappeared. For example, midway through Hartley's accounts of his Italian tour a section ends, "Some notes can be inserted here," followed by statements of such immediacy and specificity as would seem unavailable from sheer memory ("Leaving Florence on the two o'clock train," etc.). On the other hand, it is unlikely that Hartley could have carried very much in the way of records to Bavaria, where he went directly after the year in Mexico. For the bulk of the manuscript, it would seem that Hartley wrote from a stimulated and awake action of memory.

Hartley associated memory and vision. Emerson's "transparent eyeball" is an apt phrase here—it is from his essay (a favorite of Hartley's) "The Oversoul" (1841) and tropes the act of seeing as the seamless path between nature and the soul, object and subject. Emerson was obsessed with the sense of sight, and likewise for Hartley references to vision and the eyes recur both as phenomena and as figures in the autobiography. In one of the very letters to his niece in which Hartley discusses "Somehow a Past," he reveals his attention to eyes in comments about the Munich Dürer self-portrait:

> Dürer seemed to have all that the eye can have, he saw things exactly as they were, and knew how to convey that impression. Never have I seen such eyes in a painting, for they seem to roll from side to side as you look into them—most portraits are an image of the outside, but this one is flesh, bone, mind all in one.

Hartley's leitmotifs in SAPI are the "boy on the second step" or the "boy in the Tapley photo," and blue eyes. (One of Hartley's additions to the table of contents for SAPI was "To the Boy on the Steps.") His own eyes, which were an unusually pale blue, offered Hartley in 1933 a metaphor for seeing—and seeing the boy in the photo, copies of which actually exist in both Yale and Bates Hartley collections, was seeing himself in the past. The figures also signify *seeing in* the past, or *seeing the past*—that is, getting its "right profile," as with a portrait of a mountain. Hartley's account of things seen and life lived was by his own account ordinary—as he wrote to Norma (appendix 2)—and special: "I have always wondered what brown eyes see because my own eyes have always been the bluest of blue."

As a "transparent eyeball," Hartley is a passive, centerless intelligence. SAPI does not provide us with a clear picture of Hartley the man—it does not function as a mirror. It does not hold forth on the state of his soul. It only gives voice to his experience. Hartley seems drawn to this idea of a centrifugal self-referentiality that leaves the self, itself, out. Along with this, and compared to other artists in the circles in which he traveled (like Picasso or Stieglitz), Hartley seems to have had limited interest in making graphic self-portraits. A unique series of self-portrait sketches done in 1908 exist, many (interestingly) with wide, staring eyes.[45] But nothing further in this genre is known until 1939—a year in which he was probably rewriting his autobiography.[46] And then there is a strange symbolic painting, *The Sustained Comedy (Portrait of an Object)*, now in the Carnegie Institute in Pittsburgh. The image, as iconic as Dürer's, has Hartley's facial features, although enhanced with makeup and bleached blond hair, and an un-Hartleylike muscular tattooed body.

Like that of Dürer, Hartley's self-portrait contains references to Christ, and, more, the Christlike condition of martyrdom. The painting has convincingly been described as an expression of Hartley's homosexuality, and the arrows that pierce his eyes have been suggested as references to St. Sebastian, traditionally a kind of patron saint of gay men.[47] This may be true, but St. Sebastian usually has arrows in his abdomen, not his eyes. That type of maiming is more oedipal than homosexual, and, given Hartley's unhappy childhood, invites a wealth of psychoanalytical speculation. But rit-

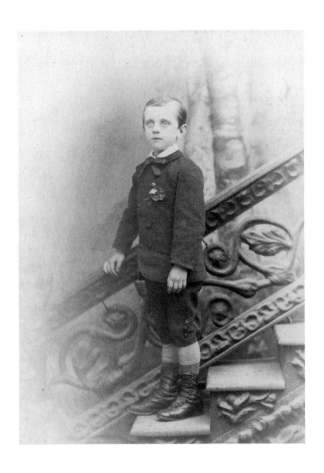

Photo of Hartley at about age 7 by [?] Larock,
Lewiston, Maine, ca. 1884. Marsden Hartley
Collection, Yale Collection of American Literature,
Beinecke Rare Book and Manuscript Library,
Yale University.

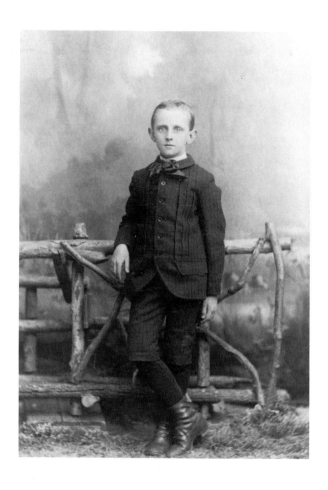

Photo of Hartley at about age 8 by I. S. Tapley,
Lewiston, Maine, ca. 1885. Marsden Hartley
Collection, Yale Collection of American Literature,
Beinecke Rare Book and Manuscript Library,
Yale University.

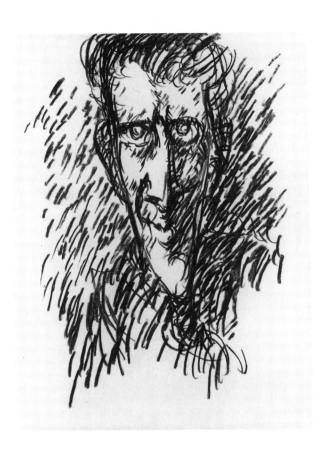

Hartley, *Self Portrait,* 1908, ink on paper, private
collection, San Francisco.

ual figures with pierced eyes are also common imagery in pre-Columbian painting that Hartley would have encountered in Mexico.[48] Whatever the source, what we have here is Hartley, with his very pale blue eyes into which arrows have been plunged, and on his forehead, an occultish triangle hit by a bolt of lightning. His "likeness" here, which tropes his presence, is countered by his blindness, signifying absence, and echoes a theme that intermittently surfaced in earlier letters (between 1929 and 1933), as when he wrote to Rebecaa Strand, "My main trouble this period is a passionate desire to eliminate myself. I don't want to be the object of self interest that one is supposed to be." [49]

On the other hand, as in the Dürer, so here, the specular eye of self-portraiture always implies a blind spot, a lapse: "Seeing the seeing and not the visible, it sees nothing," as Derrida puts it.[50] Hartley is an "object" here because he cannot see. Furthermore, in his self-portrait, like blind Oedipus, Hartley has the spark of imagination or intuition (the lightning bolt) but is denied the gift of sight. On the back of the painting Hartley wrote the word "Travesty." Prominently displayed on Hartley's shirt in the painting is a crucified Christ that resembles a painting he did later, in 1942—both paintings seem to refer to the death of Alty and Donny Mason, sons in the family Hartley had lived with in Nova Scotia, an event that hit him hard and paralleled his loss of the German officer over three decades earlier.[51] Hartley was moved to paint himself at that moment in 1939 as an expression of mourning. But he has gathered his symbols and allusions together in a picture of ritual blinding.

Ongoing Autobiography

In 1939, Hartley had already begun rewriting "Somehow a Past," generating manuscripts with subtitles that now suggest an openly organized, ongoing writing practice: "A Sequence of Memories Not to Be Called an Autobiography" (SAP2), and "A Journal of Recollection" (SAP3). These later versions can be dated substantially between 1936 and 1943.[52] He may have worked on them during any of several periods in later years in which he recorded being absorbed in literary work, as in a letter to Norma, dated August 31, 1937:

Georgetown [Maine] is a little sleepy. There are advantages, however—complete peace—wonderful for living and working and have re-written my msses [sic] . . . over 60,000 words and a lot of new poems.[53]

In 1937, three years after his return from Bavaria, it is easy to imagine that the 60,000 words of manuscript might have included, besides essays and poems, the start of a new version of "Somehow a Past." Or, perhaps, some work took place during the spring and summer of 1941, in Corea, Maine, and in New York City. This was a self-described literary period in which we know he revised and typed the prose elegy based on the Mason family tragedy, "Cleophas on His Own," and worked on an essay collection, "The Spangle of Existence."[54] But because of internal references to places or publications, the bulk of the later "Somehow a Past" versions can be dated to the last three or four years of his life in his native Maine. For example, from SAP2:

> boats plying between New York and Portland . . . [are] . . . no longer in service, else those of us who like boats could enjoy the coastal run from Portland up to Eastport and Lubec—stopping at all the Maine ports such as Belfast—Castine which is across the river from where I write this. As I look out the window, I see the sardine factory over at Castine, across the Bagaduce River.

In this case, the reference to the scene of writing dates the piece to 1939, when he spent the summer—doing much writing—with John and Clair Evans, Mabel Dodge's son and daughter-in-law, in West Brookville, Maine, from where he could have had the view described.[55]

In general, the manuscripts designated here as SAP2 and SAP3 are more fragmentary, less organized, and less single-minded than SAP1. The later pieces add only occasional bits of new information, such as his early job in New York, working as an extra in productions at Proctor's Theater in Harlem. Many more pages are taken up with reruns and amplifications of episodes already described in SAP1 like Stieglitz's 291 luncheons and Mabel Dodge's soirées in New York. However, the real focus of the later versions is Hartley's youth, and he starts his life story again and again at the beginning.

It is unclear as to whether or not Hartley thought of himself as revising, or replacing, the 1933 manuscript, and equally unclear whether or not he even had that manuscript at hand, since SAP2 and SAP3 also omit much that SAP1 contained. Perhaps Hartley did not have a plan; perhaps the original manuscript simply initiated a long-term practice of autobiographical writing, in which he turned over and over certain key episodes like his Maine childhood and his first job at the marble office in Cleveland. The pattern of repetition and return throughout all the manuscripts, taken together, implies intense psychological motivations, but it also accords with his artistic practice. Just as he worked over and over at the profiles or "portraits" of mountains, he worked at "getting right" his portraits of the past.

Old age plays havoc with short-term recall but often agitates memories of youth. Hartley was only in his early sixties when he rewrote the autobiography, but he was aging quickly as his health rapidly failed. His ruminations churn up vivid new details of old stories. In SAP3 he writes:

I remember that as small ones we used to go skating on the outer edges of the Androscoggin above the falls—to the left[?] bank—for in the middle the elders of the town carried on horse racing and I can still see the flickers of crushed ice flying from their hooves—while on the other bank of the river—great blocks of ice 18 inches thick were being towed into ice houses filled with sawdust—and all this was brought back once again on the Kenduskeag River at Bangor this last winter.

This must have been written in 1940 or 1941, after the two winters Hartley spent in Bangor.

But at certain significant times his memory fails, ironically, and key episodes in his life are repeatedly forgotten, omitted, or displaced in all versions of "Somehow a Past." There is no clear memory of his mother, Eliza Horbury, who died when he had just turned eight (about the time of the Tapley photo), in 1885. She was buried on March 4 of that year, an event Hartley recalls wrongly. He dates it from President Garfield's inaugura-

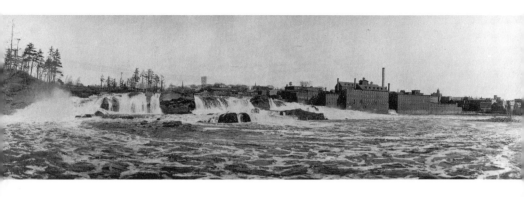

"Androscoggin Falls, Lewiston, Maine,"
stereoscopic photograph. Marsden Hartley
Collection, Yale Collection of American Literature,
Beinecke Rare Book and Manuscript Library,
Yale University.

tion—that had taken place on March 4, 1881—or perhaps with Garfield's assassination a few months later in 1881. But in his autobiographical writings, Hartley reports very detailed memories of the mills on the Androscoggin River in Lewiston, Maine, where his father worked, and even the sound of the looms and the rushing water. He remembers his first classes in school. He says he could still feel the draft that came out of the family's horsehair parlor, and see the Landseer engravings on the walls, and the rosewood piano he once scratched with a pin, but of his mother there is only a void. "I remember little—almost nothing of my mother." Over the years he wrote such statements again and again in later fragments of "Somehow a Past," and likewise his mother is barely mentioned in an autobiographical poem, "The Red Plush Family Album," published in 1940.[56]

His mother's image is consistently displaced by intensely clear images that function like screen memories. One is his insistence (despite the facts) upon the simultaneity of the Garfield tragedy. Another is the poignant story of the white kitten—an episode not found in the 1933 manuscript but repeated several times in the later ones. In this event, he and his sister buried an "early symbol," as he calls the kitten, in a salt box in Lewiston's Franklin pasture, bordered by a "stream of clean water," and engulfed with flowers: trillium, Jack-in-the-pulpit, and white and blue violets. White flowers form a frequent motif in all three manuscripts.

Likewise, among his vivid recollections of Germany no explicit mention is made of the human subject of his German Officer portraits, Hartley's beloved Lieutenant von Freyburg who died in World War I. Instead, there are colorful descriptions of Alice Miriam Pinch, an opera diva and another member of Hartley's Berlin circle, who also died tragically young. He refrains from describing the more personal tragedy, just as his keepsake portraits of Freyberg avoid the facial likeness.

Similarly, in SAPI Hartley omits the story of Hart Crane's suicide from his own account of Mexico. Hartley had met Crane in 1929 in Marseilles, and saw him several times three years later in Mexico, where Crane happened to be at the time. Crane, who was scheduled to sail home earlier than Hartley, flung himself over the railing of his steamship and died at sea, one of the most famous suicides in American letters. The event deeply affected

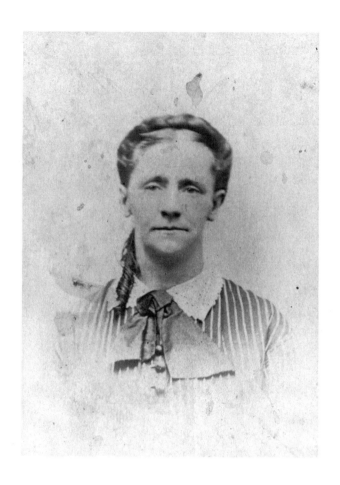

Eliza Jane Horbury (Hartley's mother), ca. 1880,
Marsden Hartley Collection, Yale Collection of
American Literature, Beinecke Rare Book and
Manuscript Library, Yale University.

Hartley. He treated it at length elsewhere, in painting, poetry, and prose.[57] Despite its emotional aspect, or maybe because of it, Hartley omitted it from his own life story. To such intimate sorrows the spectator-autobiographer is blind.

The analogy Hartley made between memory and vision remained throughout the later writings. In all the central feature of Hartley's autobiographical approach is the connection of memory, or remembered experience, and vision. In SAP2—penned between 1939 and 1941—he compares his memory to "a roll of coloured film which I can unroll at any moment." But he also turns back to the idea of the original manuscript, and to the subjects of Leonardo and mountains.

> I began the original form of "Somehow a Past" with the usual beginning I was born and all that . . . I wanted to follow . . . what I have since learned from Leonardo's notes was the right way to express mountains, and that was by getting the contours of these heights in the exact ratio to their immensity because without these contours there would be no shape at all merely bulk. . . . if a perfect picture is retained of what we really remember then this will somehow suffice to furnish a profile at least of what really happens to one: and so it is this quality that comes out in most private histories—there is seldom more than a calligraphic outline, a profile, a silhouette.

Or, as Hartley expressed it in SAP3, also just a few years before he died:

> It is not with love or with pity that we understand everything, it is with pure perception—clean insight into what makes the movements of every man—any man—*his* movements.[58]

Representing "Somehow a Past"

Ultimately, the most important distinction between SAP1 and the other "Somehow a Past" manuscripts is the scene of writing. This scene binds the manuscript to a particular time and place, documented in Hartley's letters to his niece. It lays to rest the confusion presented by the existence of the several differently organized manuscripts. There is a logic. We need only accept that SAPI, the most complete manuscript and the one with internal references to circumstances around 1933 (for example, in his discussion of fascism in Italy he writes that he is "in Germany or Bavaria at the moment"), was also the one Hartley described in his letters as it was being written. Furthermore, it was only this particular version (SAPI) that someone, most likely Norma, chose to type out. The other manuscripts are difficult to circumscribe completely in terms of time and place of writing. But they are undoubtedly later, and turn the initial alpine autobiography project into a continuous practice that lasted the rest of Hartley's life.

The scene of writing is an intense one with certain influences and particular goals: to capture past experience without getting bogged down in emotions or self-analysis. SAPI was conceived in response to a piece of avant-garde literature, *The Autobiography of Alice B. Toklas,* but also as an essentially private document. In November 1933 it was a means to pass a lonely time, and yet it engaged the very system of beliefs that energized his painting and his attitude toward life. In preparing the presentation of SAPI, I have sought to respect the principles of factuality and authenticity, but without getting embroiled in the potentially unending task to which these principles can lead. I have taken reasonable steps to ensure that the manuscript as it exists, with imperfections that naturally followed from the author's haste and subsequent unsettled lifestyle, does not produce a barrier to its own delights.

Naturally the manuscript in Hartley's own handwriting, not the typescript version, which is inaccurate in many details and overall the less coherent of the two, provided the source for this text. In transcribing this manuscript for readers, I have followed the thrust of editorial precedent regarding Hartley manuscripts, but I have also made some significant departures.[59] A compromise had to be established concerning Hartley's characteristic running prose style, a style that is punctuated by abundant dashes, occasional illegal semicolons, and all-too-rare periods. These are idiosyncratic habits that Hartley formed early in life and do not seem to be the result of influence from Gertrude Stein, who rarely used dashes, even in manuscript. As Gail Scott points out, Hartley often corrected his overuse of dashes when he typed his own manuscripts for publication.[60] But just how he corrected them is difficult to pin down as a system. The autobiographical manuscripts were not typed by Hartley and never clearly envisioned by him as a final finished product. However, his unique punctuation style did create a certain rhythm of energy and emphasis, most evident in SAPI. For example, characteristically, he began a sentence with a short clause, followed by a dash and then successive clauses that transform or expand the initial thought in a way that parallels the piecemeal, progressive—and sometimes convoluted—temporal structure of memory. In general, I have tried to preserve something of this residue of energy and process, and I have left the original text's dashes where they do not impede the flow of the narrative. Furthermore, I have made other punctuation and grammatical changes as necessary to enhance that flow.

Likewise, in the original manuscript Hartley often, though not always, began each new sentence on a new line. And he seems not to have demarcated paragraphs, although there are exceptions to both these rules. Once again, for clarity, I have broken the text into paragraphs in the places where it would be natural to do so. In three places in the original manuscript, the page numbering changes or begins again at I. In the following text, a rule indicates these junctures.

Where Hartley crossed out a word, phrase, or segment in the manuscript, it was usually to rewrite the same word or idea in a different way. The emendations are clearly in Hartley's hand. These crossings-out have been entirely omitted and Hartley's changes employed in the text that follows. Hartley's handwriting, as he himself reminded Norma, is very difficult to read, and occasionally words remain illegible, or their readings questionable. This is indicated by [?].

Hartley tended to follow some British spellings consistently, such as the "our" ending of words like colour or the "re" of words like theatre. He favored extasy over ecstasy. I have kept to these idiosyncrasies. Hartley used the plus sign (+) as often as "and." I have consistently used the latter. Hartley often—not always—kept the adjectival form of nationalities in lower case, while capitalizing the noun form. This has been corrected in accordance with American practice. Often he misspelled foreign names and omitted accent marks. These too have been corrected. Hartley used quotation marks both for publication titles, and to enclose dialogue passages. In both cases, he occasionally neglected to insert or complete these, and I have done so for him.

Finally, since SAPI was a private document, Hartley provided minimal explanation for names of people and places. Some of these are now better known, others much more obscure, than in Hartley's day. Endnotes to the text are both documentary and annotative, intended to assist the general reader without unnecessarily impeding appreciation of Hartley's prose.

The guiding principle throughout this edition of Hartley's writing has been to achieve better clarity and a degree of transparency to the text without sacrificing its sense of rapid and spontaneous process. It was this sense of process that most distinguishes Hartley's goal, in art as in life: to seek the elusive imprint of action, the "calligraph" or profile of memory, and not to fix an impossibly finished picture of a life.

"SOMEHOW A PAST" [1]

Plain, simple, simple, plain,
out o the wind—in home again;
What did I see—what did I do
something to write home of—sing of
to you—
Cross 'tween a circus and sacred affair,
that left me with head floating in
multiple air—
I saw it all through a groove in the sky,
melodious experience swimming by.

It was light, it was dark, it was
morning
at midnight, it was glory through thunder
and a flash of bright winning
from the stones that fell under
and a rush of whispered beginning.

Took what there was, went on a way—
rolled ball up hill—then rolled it hill down
Saw what was gathered from Monday
to Sunday—
Went on a spree as thin as an arrow
sped like a windshift through town
after town.

Not to know why—not even to know—
just had to be as had then to go;
Lightning like changes in all the vast
range
of the pieces that fell in a place to regain
mirrored sense of each triplicate change
lose, gain, lose, then something remain.

Turned then about to a length of the east

Turned then about to a length of the west

Let the ray fall from the steel coloured

north—

through the touch of the flame of the

burning south—

and here—the slight toy at its mid

morning worth.

The alchemy fell on the disc of the

dream

mingled with moments of shimmering

sun,

and therefore—the plain theme of one.

SOMEHOW A PAST
Prologue to Imaginative Living

I was christened Edmund, with no other name to accentuate it—1877. I should have I think now been proud of this name as it was that of an uncle who appears vaguer to me in vision than my father, but by the aid of a photograph I recognize a handsome man.

I never thought of eliminating this name, but for sentimental reasons I inserted the family name of our stepmother who had endeared herself to us by sharing her life with my father—whom she had known back in childhood as also my mother. They all emigrated to Lewiston, Maine, when there was the habit to emigrate as it still is with peoples like the Finnish and the Swedish though conditions in their countries are far more idealistic now than they were then. My mother Eliza Horbury died at the close of my eighth year—and of her I have little or no recollection. I see the face laboured with agonies of last illness—but I hear no voice and see no gesture—and the little I know of her came to me from my five sisters in whose life she placed a complete part.

March 4th, 1888 was, I think, the day of the assassination of President Garfield and the burial day of my mother.[1] The life which began for me was settled at that moment and I was to know complete isolation from that moment onward. I was of course "cared" for but naturally through the transferred maternity of a particular sister who remained, and probably for that reason alone, particularly near to me.[2] I remember her singing to me a song so completely fatal in its effect but was probably in vogue then for whatever reason—and the song was—"All all alone—alone in a dungeon cell," and the rest I either forgot or did not probably memorize.[3]

I do remember I was shy to an exaggerated degree—said to be energetic enough—though later to become subject to most of the floating children's ills and made frail by them. But as I lived an entirely imaginative life of my own—no one that I can recall figured to any marked degree save the sister already spoken of. The household was broken up and my two sisters then unmarried eventually went to Cleveland, Ohio, to live with an older sister married to a dashing young man from Danbury, Connecticut, who wore a fashionable beard and a coat with a fur collar with a fur hat. The photograph provides this image from the red plush family album, with the word *album* in Spencerian scroll fastened to the cover.[4]

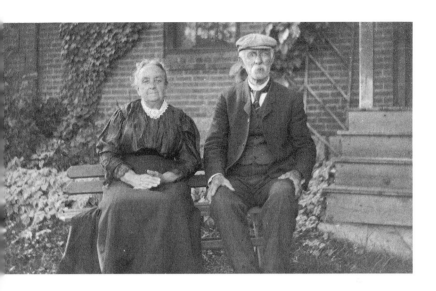

Martha Marsden Hartley (Marsden Hartley's
stepmother) and Thomas Hartley (his father), date
unknown, Marsden Hartley Collection, Yale
Collection of American Literature, Beinecke Rare
Book and Manuscript Library, Yale University.

I remember a few moments of history in a primary school in Bates Street, Lewiston, a large red brick affair with two sides and two entrances—one for girls and one for boys. As the boys' side all looked at the granite wall of the chancel of Trinity Church—Episcopalian of course—and through wire gratings to protect the glass, the image of the Ascension could be made out. On exit from that school I was to become a member of the choir of said granite church and sang alto. The organist was a plump woman with much superfluous hair on her face and a nervous twitching in her eyes—the organ being like all others of the period, pumped by hand.

With the entrance into the grammar school I had a long walk and most of it lay along a wooded piece in the Franklin pasture known to us all, and even now is known to the children, as a vast place full of wonder.[5] The school building had a cupola and of course a bell—and I used to hurry during the spring period, in advance to this wooded piece, because a brook ran through it and in this brook were the usual water plants and especially a lot of watercress dear to the appetites of the English especially since it is a favorite in England and my parents were of course English. It is said that my mother had to hurry home from a visit to England as she wished me to be a Yankee boy as otherwise I might have mechanically become an English one if I had been born on an English ship. I have been to the section of England where all my people came from—namely Lancashire on the border of Yorkshire and the Yorkshire moors, and as I am now reading "Wuthering Heights" over again at this juncture—I can see vaguely the brim of Rochdale and of Dewsbury—the latter figuring in the biography of the Brontë family for obvious reasons.[6] These moors have been made still more memorable to me in the life of that engaging first mystic of England, Richard Rolle, who wrote precious songs to his Jhesu, living among the rocks of those famous Yorkshire moors—and one day I wanted to foot it over those moors to fill in a full experience of what is but a faint wisp of memory.

In this same community Francis Thompson was born, the son of a doctor, who was to endure such tragic experience in his flight from reality—the flight leading him to face reality itself as few have ever faced it with more terrible consequences, which will be unfolded in the book by

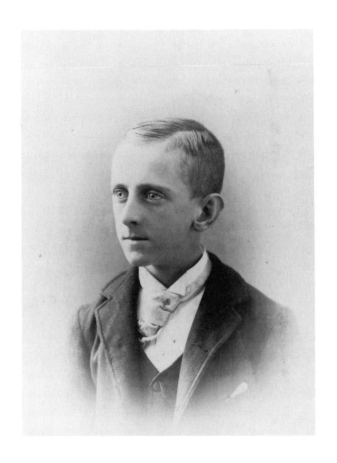

Photo of Hartley at about age 10 by I. L.
Hammond, Lewiston, Maine, ca. 1887. Marsden
Hartley Collection, Yale Collection of American
Literature, Beinecke Rare Book and Manuscript
Library, Yale University.

Thompson. But for the deep heart of the Maynell family, "The Hound of Heaven" might never have been written and that would have been a stupendous privation.[7] I knew a man until he died who, being the same sort of a derelict with a poetic nature, but no gift for expression, remembered encountering Thompson in the bead house of London where he would wander after pawing over the garbage cans behind hotels and after selling his eleven pence worth of matches at stage doors which was the vast income of this last great mystical poet.

The flowers in this wooded piece I have spoken of, on my way to school, were magical and I owe I think nearly everything to them though I recognize them always in the botany books as trillium, jack-in-the-pulpit, dog tooth violet—and of course the usual blue violet and the white violet guarded over by false Solomon's seal and the rest. Then the bell would ring and drown out the music of falling water and I would find myself in class.

I can see the teachers as vividly now as then but I see them more gently now as they were then a little terrifying. I see the very classroom—and a boy in the next row always impressed me by his natural energy and masculine signatures and this boy grew up to be Senator Wallace H. White of Maine who still performs that office.[8] I can see a pale girl with a sharp Yankee tongue and corn colored hair who in later life proved to be an excellent accompanist and was for years the accompanist of Emilio de Gogorza, husband of Emma Eames.[9] Frank Holding, who turned out to be an excellent violinist and was on tour with Lillian Nordica when she died in Batavia, was I think in a class ahead of me or he must have been behind me surely—as Professor Fred Pomeroy was to be one class ahead of me and who was to become professor of zoology at Bates College, which office he has held throughout his life and still presides in this capacity.[10]

Fred will tell you how I related to him that in grammar school days I had taken a dislike to him in childish fashion—as he too like Wallace White was strong, energetic, and forward. We talk now when we meet of the later friendship and of how I used to sit with him in his room reading something or other while he was plugging for Harvard—and he is still the same fine person that he was then.

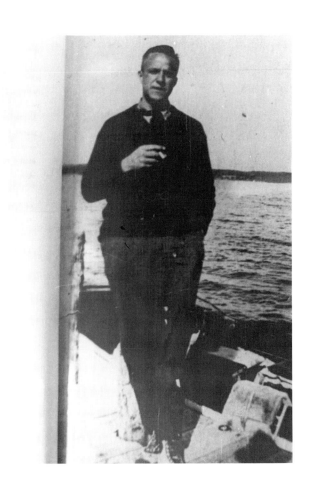

Wallace Gould in Maine, ca. 1925, courtesy of
Longwood College, Farmville, Virginia.

It was on return visits that I made the acquaintance of Wallace Gould the poet, who was to give me the pleasure of making him known to the poets Alfred Kreymborg and William Carlos Williams, who praised Gould's poetry for its solid execution and a true modernist touch, and who was a fanatical worshiper of Byron.[11]

Gould began life as a child prodigy at the piano and for some unknown reason gave up the idea of becoming a public pianist and for years afterward played the piano in the first period of the silent pictures. Gould was physically enormous—weighing two hundred pounds which his six feet one carried with ease. He was by nature a voluptuary—oriental even in his worship of luxury and food—was an excellent cook and often cooked elaborate meals after work at night, sharing this of course with friends—the cooking itself being the chief delight. He was handsome with olive skin suffused with warm red, glowing eyes, and dark hair—and was he said some sort of cousin to Holman Day who has written many local ballads—appealing chiefly to plain taste, a sort of downeast Edgar Guest—giving the simple picture with the homely sentiment pervading it.[12]

Gould lived with and supported a foster mother and the lifelong grind at the piano earning twenty-five a week was an exhausting self-imposed duty—but he stayed until things took a turn, then left the white house with the green blinds and never returned. No one has heard of him for years though rumour has it he went south, married eventually, and scorned all chance of publicity either as poet or as person. He has become a self-created *soldat inconnu* in keeping his own secret under the perpetual flame.

Gould had sweep—he was an intense egotist. Pride was almost a disease with him. Yet he was the epitome of warmth and kindness. I used to sit behind him during my weekly visit to my father in Lewiston—at the theatre—which he implored to me to do. "I go nearly crazy grinding out that stuff day after day—I get a kick out of it if someone sits behind me." It was always remarked next day how marvelously he played—and he was fond of Liszt who was so suited to his own type of emotional flamboyance.

Wallace Gould was cynical for natural reasons—he had been crucified by the pressure of duty. He could not leave the woman who had rescued him from the fate of orphanage—he loved her—called her his mother all his life—and she had mothered dozens of children like so many women who cannot have children of their own. He was a great reader of the classics, but he declined to show interest in any of the moderns. It tortured him to know I was at that stage reading Whitman, to whom he had a vague resemblance though he was in no sense democratic in his interests or appreciations—being essentially and haughtily patrician to the point almost of mania.

I left grammar school at fifteen to go to work and from that moment on the fight began that was to bring me to the pitch of the present. As my father and stepmother decided to go to Cleveland, to join the rest of the family, I boarded with my sister in Auburn, Maine, and worked in the office of a shoe factory at the breath-taking salary of three dollars a week—checking up on the lots as they passed through from one department to another. The price for labour was so much a pair—the worker keeping a check book, and this was passed in at evening to be verified according to the lot sheets and the books put back into the rack in the hall where the workers could take them out of the rack in the morning on the way to work.

After a year or so of that it was decided that I should go to Cleveland too—and there we were all united—three sisters, Martha and father, and myself. I found employment in the office of a marble quarry on the Cuyahoga River—a stream almost as muddy as the Rio Grande save that the Rio Grande was clean seepage from the age old chasms, whereas the Cuyahoga was dingy and thick with just plain dirt. But it could take in barges and vessels and so much shipping was carried on on this river.

Again I enjoyed the magnificent stipend of three dollars a week—sweeping out the upstairs office and running errands for the superintendent down in the works. I was in constant association then with huge blocks of valuable marbles from the quarters of the earth. So my daily tasks brought me in touch with Pavanazzo, which is a beautiful marble of rich honey yellow veined with purple black, verde antique, which was a handsome green like peat moss veined with whitish veins, and a very pleasant foil to Numidian, which was a glowing dark Pompeian red. And there was of course Carrara and the regular beautiful granites—all these being used in finishing off the halls of office buildings for facings both outer and counter for banks, and all these three [sic] marbles are extremely handsome.

There was of course onyx with its sort of opalish moonstonelike quality, never quite translucent but as if windows could be made of it. That idea was employed in the cathedral windows in Orvieto in Italy, as if to sort of copy the colour of the native wine which is the colour of their honey—seductively sweet and with a heady force that amazes—even though it tastes so velvety when it is first drunk. I sometimes think that my aesthetic tastes were finally and definitely aroused by contact with those wonderful marbles of which there were always choice specimens in the office to show to prospective builders.

I never see these marbles in new buildings now and I assume that glass has been substituted, mostly black because it is cheaper and because importation from Italy and Africa made the marble expensive. But I do see these marbles in modern desk service as bases for fountain pens—and onyx comes in here frequently because it is decorative and appealing whereas it has gone out of lampstand employment since streamline introductions.

So from the period in which I was born—of the horse hair furniture in a set [?] stuffy parlor with the rosewood piano—a Chickering it was—with Landseer engravings on the walls in black polished frames with a fine gilt edge next to the engraving setting it off—with the pale brown spots running here and there in the paper on which the engravings were printed, denoting the action of the air upon the binding substance in the paper—some sort of glue emulsion I assume—as all papers, the most ancient ones have it whereas one never remarks it now as the chemical process is very different and it is the era of stockings made of spun wood—to the Pavanazzo-Numidian-verde antique of the marble factory, so I have made a step in taste, and love of flowers and sunshine did the rest.

I began somehow to have curiosity about art at the time when sex consciousness is fully developed and as I did not incline to concrete escapades I of course inclined to abstract ones, and the collecting of objects which is a sex expression took the upper hand. I have no way of recalling who took me to the old City Hall building on Superior Street where there were some gloomy looking art studios on the top floor—to meet John

Semon, landscape painter of the Barbizon persuasion and by no means a bad painter. He was a sort of self-invented cross between Corot and Theodore Rousseau—smoked his pipe incessantly and painted as I recall nothing but beach woods with their golden bark and spreading roots embedded in luscious mosses.

Semon planted the art virus in my soul. I had become inoculated and the virus took. The next step was the meeting of Nina Waldeck, who was teaching the antique in the Cleveland School of Art—after I had arranged with the marble office to have Monday morning off to study still life with Semon at one dollar a lesson, which I had to work two days to earn—three dollars being the return for six days labour. I began to learn to pound a typewriter, a Blickendorfer. I recall it perfectly, with the letters arranged in a drum which when pressed by the keys would pound down the desired letter—and of course only by the "hunt and peck" two finger system which I never did progress from though I write very decently now with it. Of course it is the entirely wrong system as one must never think of the keys.

I went on two weeks' vacation with Semon down to his woods in southerly Ohio somewhere, the place and other circumstances escaping me. Neither do I recall by what means I had established my eligibility for entrance into art classes but I remember the rest of the course, and never shall I forget the face and distinction of Miss Waldeck, who was to mean everything for later development because she was a real artist through and through though like so many good teachers her own work never quite came through. But she at least did get to Spain and copied Velásquez in the Prado.[13]

I lost my job in the marble office because, I suspect, Mr. Dygert the superintendent saw the downfall coming and that I never would be any good to him—in the marble business or any other business.

A very blond pink young man of manners of the suave hue came to Cleveland "direct from Paris" to establish a summer class—and of course he had painted the French countryside in a sort of half hearted impressionist way. He invited me to his summer class and in the fall gave an exhibition of his pupils' work and courteously called the attention of one of the trustees to my little labours. This wealthy lady was Miss Anne Walworth, with

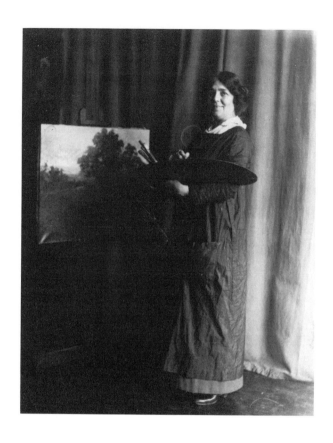

Nina Waldeck, Marsden Hartley Collection, Yale
Collection of American Literature, Beinecke Rare
Book and Manuscript Library, Yale University.

a mansion in what was then magnificent Euclid Avenue with its extensive lawns allowing each house almost a park to itself—along with the Wades and the politically inclined Mark Hanna family and whomever else formed the upper crust of society at that time.

The art school was in a discarded mansion of what was then known as Wilson Avenue. Cleveland was well out to give itself a name as a center of good taste and from this nucleus of rich patrons the now very beautiful museum was organized in the new section of Cleveland. The East End had been set as the right place to live—the decline and fall of one of the most beautiful avenues in this country had begun—which is now in pitiful state to one who remembers the grandeur and elegance of that epoch.

It was arranged through Miss Walworth's interest that I was to go to New York to school, and I was to have four hundred and fifty dollars a year for study—of which three hundred were for winter schooling and one hundred fifty for summer, and these sums were separately forwarded me for five years. Instead of returning to Cleveland in the summer I returned to Lewiston, Maine, my birthplace. In that epoch was formed the fine friendship of Professor Fred Pomeroy of Bates College—who is as distinguished in appearance as a professor as he was as a student preparing for post graduate work at Harvard, for Fred has always been a handsome fellow.

I met also Alice Farrar and she too was interested in art and had studied in Portland in the school operated by Charles Fox and Curtis Perry, both artists who had studied in Europe at Julian's or Beaux Arts or both.[14] Both were men of means—both startling the staid correct and rich world of Portland by adopting some aspect of socialism—dressing in sackcloth and ashes so to speak and were the renegades of a well-founded, smug, well-born, well-bred element, which gave Portland its distinction and of which it retains a surprising degree of elegance to this day though many of the grand mansions look disconsolate now. I indicate all this by an experience last winter in a better class restaurant when a lady in elegant black—much white powder on her already whitened cheeks and the faint sound of jet about her person—said to me, "How shocked my father would be if he knew I were eating in a restaurant." And this restaurant is full of just this

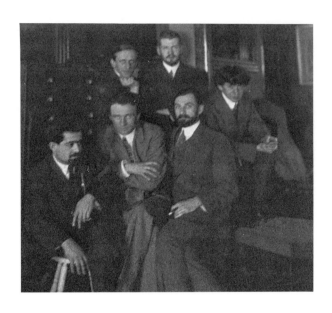

"A group of young American Artists of the Modern
School," 1911, Marsden Hartley Memorial
Collection, Museum of Art, Bates College. Top (left
to right): Hartley, Lawrence Fellows, John Marin;
Bottom (left to right): Jo Davidson,
Edward Steichen, Arthur B. Carles.

sort of aging ladies and gentlemen whose fortunes have dwindled and the servant problem has become generally prohibitive, no second maids or butlers in evidence now.

Fox and Perry had a summer rendezvous at North Bridgeton on the upper ridge. That is, they arranged to live with a young farmer and his wife—she to cook the meals and each to do his own room work as according to the new conscience each must take his share of labour. But all this was to be had for four dollars a week, with a thrilling view of the near White Mountains and a group of curiously interesting people—and Gertie Adams was an excellent cook.

I never saw Charles Fox paint but Curtis Perry used to paint dozens of little panels of cherry-wood with nervous, superficial, glowing half impressionistic studies, chiefly of the special aspects of nature like spring blossoming, rainbows, and autumn flame—and many paintings of mushrooms were made, all of course to satisfy science and not to express any new esthetic impulse. Perry was a single track man then and the subject was butterflies and he had an amazing collection of expensive specimens for I distinctly recall that one of them—all iridescent like Phoenician glass—cost fifteen dollars. But the object was of course the study of colour and design and hobbies were necessary to those who had a great deal of money and who hadn't earned it—as it is today.

"291"[15]

This room was probably the largest small room of its kind in the world—certainly then—probably now.

Everybody in the wide world came there sooner or later—everybody was free to come. It was an open room—and anyone said what he liked. Many times it was interesting—sometimes not—but no matter what anyone thinks of that room now—and the succeeding rooms with the numbers 303 and 1710[16]—this room 291 left a lasting impression in the development of art in America and no other room has had precisely this meaning or precisely this effect. It was a big room and it entertained the world regardless of class or station. Nobody was left out of it—the coloured elevator boy whose name was Hodge became something to it—and Marie the secretary was distinctly a figure in the whole scheme.

There were scoffers who came to scorn and scoff either at the pictures or Stieglitz or both—and there were the believers who came to believe in both.

Alfred Stieglitz is an extraordinary person—and by that I mean he has had many sides to his nature. He was a racetrack hound, a musician, a billiard player, and still is the world's greatest photographer. The photography of Stieglitz was a great aid to all of us for it had the same effect on the painters as the intense realism of Courbet had on the impressionists who were swinging out widely yet always coming back to Courbet. A Stieglitz photograph—and I am sure I am speaking for the other painters of the group as well as for myself—had the effect of making us see nature better—I always felt so at least—and I still believe a good photograph is better than a bad painting.

Stieglitz had special generosities which I fear were far less beneficial to him. He maintained his lunch table at the Holland House for many years—and he had many of us at his home for years also. He took as many as there were to lunch at noon—and he took whomever he wanted home with him to dinner and to some concert usually after. It was in the domestic routine of Stieglitz to do all these things. Otherwise his life was excessively simple—and admitted to no ostentation of any kind. He shared with his associates whatever he had—and he had the specially outstanding quality of never once suggesting, certainly not to me ever in all the years I was in the group, never saying why do you do this—why don't you do that. He seemed to know that what we all did was natural to us. He knew that our lives called for a certain scale—that each lived in his own scale—that it cost each one so much a year to live his way and work his way—and set to work accordingly to set us all to work knowing that work made us happy and that we were not fooling our time away or bluffing in any way ourselves or him. The understanding was perfect. He knew that one needed to go somewhere—that another needed to be still.

He knew that I was a traveler—and that my education lay out in the open free areas of the world—and that I must go wherever my education

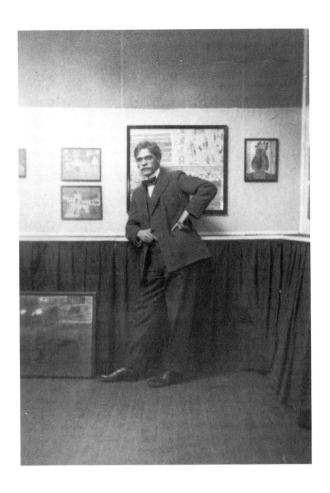

Stieglitz at 291, Alfred Stieglitz Collection, Yale
Collection of American Literature, Beinecke Rare
Book and Manuscript Library, Yale University. He
poses with his exhibition of children's drawings,
held at the gallery in the spring of 1912, just about
the time Hartley left for Europe.

called for me to go. What an extraordinary condition it was—unique surely in the world of artists—one man understanding and believing in a number of outstanding types and seeing to it that they could live and work and produce more work. Only the insiders, we ourselves could know what this meant, and because all of us were clothed, fed, and at work—we were all supposed to be rich—and of course we were rich—anybody who is clothed, fed, and kept warm is rich. I at least look back on all this now and I say—what miracle. One man—one person who believed in several people all at once—and saw to it that none of these came to want.

How many other single persons have done that, I mean in the world of painting? Groups and institutions have done this and are still doing it— but not one man who among rich men was a poor man. I don't know whether Stieglitz will care for all this—but it doesn't matter—it all had to go down on the page. Whatever may be the point of view now—there is no alteration and no criticism on the part of myself and there never will be.

The room changed completely at 291—and almost everyone of the old group left it for one cause or another—some of them died, some of them changed their faith, some of them went abroad to live. The building was to be torn down—and the "room" was moved up to the Anderson Galleries—59th Street and Park Avenue, there to be called 303—and we who belonged went with it and were a part of it then. I was less in it because I was living in Paris and Berlin developing myself then and coming home at the usual intervals of about a year and a half or two years—long enough not to be too much missed. But I got to Paris before the 303 period.

———————

[I was taken] home to 1111 Madison Avenue by Stieglitz and for years after was a regular Sunday dinner guest in the Stieglitz family. Mrs. Stieglitz liked me, though she wasn't caring much for the whole of 291 otherwise I think—but I was glad she liked me—and at the Sunday dinners there was nearly always John B. Kerfoot—a fine person who wrote book reviews for "Life" and was an exceedingly well dressed man. He gave complete attention to his *complets* as the French call them, even to the shirt studs and cuff buttons—always exactly to match: amber for brown, moonstones I think for grey, and amethysts for purple, for he had a fine purple suit with a dark purple plush hat all of the most expensive importations always. Stieglitz was publishing a most expensive magazine called "Camera Work" and had all the plates done by Bruckmann of Munich—very costly it was and very perfectly done.

So it was I was a member of the Stieglitz group. It was very wonderful for all of us—because we knew we would always have a place for our exhibitions and, as it was not a commercial gallery, the tone of it was fine. We knew we could show our work and that was the main thing. The extraordinary thing was that Stieglitz knew each of us so well and knew that each case was a different case—and was treated as such—and out of each year's exhibition he somehow managed to make sales so that we could go on working for a year and a half. What an amazing condition to fall heir to— and how blessed I felt—the others did too—and it was a remarkable room all around.

Amazingly beautiful women came to these exhibitions. I can see them now coming out of the cracking of whips of the tally ho equipment that used to drive down Fifth Avenue then—and go up in the tiny elevator to see all the exhibitions. How amazing they were. I recall at least four remarkable looking women: Miss Grace Rhoades, Miss Beckett, Mrs. Agnes Meyer, and Mrs. Arthur Carles—or Mercedes de Cordoba—sister of Pedro de Cordoba, the actor—and there was also Mrs. Philip Lydig—one of the most remarkable looking women in New York.[17] They were all tall women statuesque in build—and always astonishingly dressed. I remember chiefly Mrs. Carles who was always in black and white—long white gloves, long ivory earrings—a remarkable profile—and very Spanish looking. Mrs. Lydig, also I think of Spanish origin, always wore black—and I remember one of her costumes was a black pony coat and the hat was a small coachman's derby with four small uncurled ostrich feathers falling at the side whither the leather rosette usually was in a coachman's derby.

The men were all smart and fine looking—outside of the artists, for artists were poor and wore what they were lucky enough to have—but in the European style. Nobody cared what an artist wore. "Dressing" for the artists came in with the cubists in Paris I am certain now—and that was novel for I was to see all that a little later.

Of course I wanted to go to Paris. I had seen some Matisse, Cézanne, and Picasso and I wanted to see more for I wanted to have an artist's education.

I wanted above all to see what I could see in New York and I knew Mrs. Havemeyer had several real Cézannes.[18] How to get there. It so happened a friend of Mrs. Havemeyer's used to come to 291, and she asked the beautiful woman to tea one Sunday and Arthur Carles was the other man besides myself. I spoke of this idea of seeing Mrs. Havemeyer's Cézannes then— and Mrs. Simpson said it would be easy as Mrs. Havemeyer was very kind. The matter was arranged for four people and I by a sad breach of etiquette was left out. The day came for the Havemeyer visit and the party went and my eyes got wet because I was not going. Carles said, "I am sure it is all right for you to go too," but I couldn't as I had not been personally asked and my eyes got wet. I told the story to Arthur B. Davies—and he said "O that is easy, I know Mrs. Havemeyer and I will take you,"—and he did. We were there alone—Mrs. Havemeyer leaving word with the butler she was sorry she couldn't be home—but that we must enjoy ourselves just the same.

It was an amazing afternoon—one needed strength to be with all the great pictures for everyone now knows the Havemeyer Collection in the Metropolitan Museum. I was sorry when the collection was finally put on view not to find the Cézannes I had remembered most of all. Perhaps these had been given to the family and were therefore kept out. I had had my first sweep of Cézanne and of course was all afire with the hope of getting to Paris. One day it all came like magic and I knew I could go, and there was my first voyage into the world of dreams and legend. I could go to Paris. I could have fifteen a week to live on. I knew Lee Simonson in Paris—I had known Lee from his school days—grammar school in Center Lovell.[19]

Mr. Montross Comes and Believes[20]

The special event of that first show at 291 as it comes to me was not merely the coming of everybody but the visit of Mr. N. E. Montross.[21] I make a special place for this because I have never quite had the opportunity of telling him of the effects of his interest and generosity.

Mr. Montross came down to 291 to see my show. I suppose he was more or less in the habit of going there—everybody else was. In any case Mr. Montross came and looked at the pictures and seemed interested. He invited me to go up to his gallery and visit him and said he had a picture there he would like me to see.

I went in due time and this was 550 Fifth Avenue if I am not mistaken—and I was ushered into the very still room with red plush, some easels, a few chairs, and pictures covered with pieces of red plush. Mr. Montross, with his usual sense of ceremony over pictures, took up carefully a small one and looked to be sure that I was exactly in the right place to be affected—and "to receive its message."

It was a picture that so affected me that I in all truth was never the same after the first moment—for the power that was in it shook the rafters of my being and left me sort of shaking in the force of the wind. This picture was a marine by Albert P. Ryder—just some sea, some clouds, and a sail boat on the tossing waters.

I knew little or nothing about Albert P. Ryder then—and when I learned he was from New England the same feeling came over me in the given degree as came out of Emerson's essays when they were first given to me—I felt as if I had read a page of the Bible—in both cases. All my essential Yankee qualities were brought forth out of this picture and if I needed to be stamped an American, this was the first picture that had done this—for it had in it everything that I knew and had experienced about my own New England, even though I had never lived by the sea. It had in it the stupendous solemnity of a Blake mystical picture and it had a sense of realism besides that bore such a force of nature itself as to leave me breathless. The picture had done its work and I was a convert to the field of imagination into which I was born. I had been thrown back into the body and being of my own country as by no other influence that had come to me.

The next pictures I did were solely from memory and the imagination, of which there were only four or five—those which later became known as

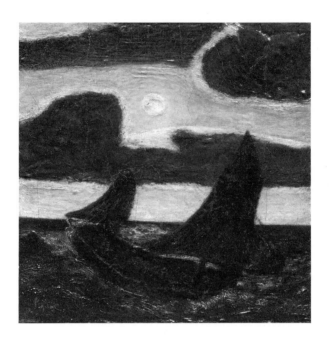

Albert Pinkham Ryder, *Moonlit Marine*, ca. 1890s,
The Metropolitan Museum of Art, New York,
Samuel D. Lee Fund, 34–55. In 1908 this painting
was in the collection of the dealer Newman E.
Montross, where Hartley would have seen it.

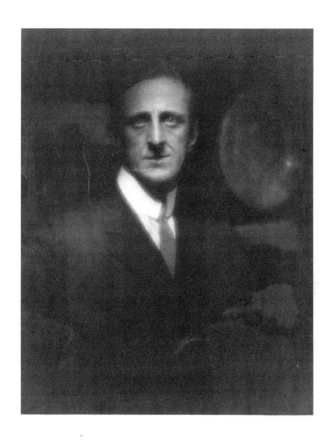

Hartley, ca. 1910, Marsden Hartley Collection,
Yale Collection of American Literature, Beinecke
Rare Book and Manuscript Library, Yale University.

the "black landscapes." All these were done in the room of Ernest Roth my school friend the etcher—who had one of the smallest of the back rooms on the top floor of 232 West 14th Street—the famous art rookery of which Alfred Kreymborg tells in his book "Troubadour"—for he was one of the rooks and had the next cage to Roth.[22]

Roth's room was full from one end to the other, with books on the sides and a printing press for etching. These rooms couldn't have been more than six feet wide and ten feet long—with a window at the back— so that in this room of Roth's with all the things in it there was just room to walk from the door to the window.

I had never lived in 232—but I had a room in one of the houses of the old Astor estate—a low row—the block long and all alike from Eighth Avenue to within a door or two of Ninth Avenue. For nine years I had a room in this home, which was then managed by Katherine Mullens and later on by Miss Mary McCarthy—two fine loyal Irish women—whose kindness to me has never been forgotten.

This section of the city had a tone of real character to it then—because it was just there that the artists lived—and a block further down it had come to be known as one of the most dangerous quarters of the city then— the hangout of the "Hudson Dusters." All those nine years of winter living at 351 West 15th—only four houses from Ninth Avenue—I never once knew or even ever heard of these gangsters or never encountered any myste- rious looking types, and there were only three gas lamps in the whole block. It was only the last year that I found myself being followed from 14th Street and Eighth Avenue—and down the block of 15th Street toward Ninth—so I turned back to a corner of Eighth Avenue again, where there was always a policeman, as I did not wish to be bagged which could easily be done because the block was long and lonesome.

Around this corner in 16th Street Albert Ryder lived in a small tene- ment. What a strange completely sequestered life. I had of course been stirred as I say by Ryder's marine and the thought of his presence round the corner was both exciting and disturbing for it seemed to be too much greatness too near—for me—and I was impelled by two intense impulses.

One was to get to see him often and know him well, the other to let him alone—which I decided to do.

Kenneth Hayes Miller was doing his portrait of Ryder somehow then.[23] But I never got used to the portrait as I never saw Ryder dressed up—and it was Ryder's custom to "dress up" once a year and go up to Fifth Avenue to "see the pictures" as he called it. Whenever I saw Ryder it was in his regular sort of grey clothes: a grey sweater, a grey skull cap, knitted—his rich full grey beard hanging down, huge shaggy eyebrows, his hands behind his back—walking up Eighth Avenue usually in the evening. We all of us ate an evening meal at Kiel's Bakery on the corner of Eighth Avenue and 15th Street—and I believe Kreymborg says Ryder ate there often also, but I never saw him there myself and I fancy he ate either earlier or later.

It was a vivid place, the bakery, and frequented mostly by men—and the men, mostly young men, were oyster openers up from Virginia. They had a pleasing accent. One of them, a blond, had more to say than the others and was more sociably inclined—and felt less inferior than they— though there was nothing to make them feel so—not in the bakery—we were all poor and serious.

Ryder's spirit lived intensely in me—and as I say I did the four or five black landscapes of that year in Roth's room. I was mourning I had no place to work for I only had a cold hall bedroom. Roth said, "If you think you can work there"—pointing to a chest against the wall—"it's all right with me." I was sure I could because Roth always had a good effect on me. I am sure he never knew it, but it is one of the silent things that make men get together and like each other—and I liked Roth and had great respect for his ardour and his indefatigable gift of industry. And so that winter the dark landscapes were done.

Mr. Montross had already asked me—how I lived and how much I lived on in the Maine woods—I said four dollars a week for food and house rent—but I had no outlook at all then. He said he would like to supply that for me for two years. I replied, "O Mr. Montross that is extremely kind of you—but you are a dealer and may be expecting something of me and I can't promise anything—I must have the right to work by myself and fail by myself." And he kindly assured me his interests were completely human—that he was sorry he couldn't do more but he would gladly do this much. So each month for two years he sent me the reckoned sum by the month, for which he refused compensation of any sort at the end of the two years—a complete gift which helped enormously to send me on my way.

I am sure I have told somewhere of the fearful squalor which wondrous Albert Ryder lived in two tiny rooms by himself—the third room piled high to the ceiling with furniture and never entered apparently.[24] The other two rooms in which he lived were a mass of debris—turned over chairs, boxes, parcels, a little stove about which were clustered heaps of ashes, oatmeal boxes, fruit and tomato cans, and a long roll of carpet on which he slept for there was no bed—and he had kept a path open among all this debris by which he could get to the window and let in air whenever he wished to. Otherwise, appalling disorder. "I never see all this," he said to me one day, "until someone comes to see me—and then I become conscious." If he expected visitors, which he now and then had, he did a little something and it seemed to look like order to him.

All this meant nothing to anyone who loved and revered Ryder the artist with as great an imagination in his way as Blake had in his—the greatest imagination in painting that America has so far produced. There are no more American artists of that type of intensity and there never will be—for Ryder closed a period in New England cultivation—he closed it with George Fuller in the world of painting.[25]

It was in these chaos ridden rooms that I saw the now well known pictures, "The Tempest" and "Macbeth." I have not seen "The Tempest" since then and the "Macbeth" was so cleaned up when I did see it that I almost failed to recognize it, because it had a grey over it which I come to think now must have been the dust of the years. And so that corner of New York had true artistic history for it was made, if by no one else, by Albert P. Ryder.

Alfred Kreymborg tells all of this in "Troubadour" and I leave it to him. He says I wore gardenias—but I am still doubting it for I was never that courageous nor am I now, enough to wear flowers in my buttonhole.

That I used to buy one or two in the spring from the Greeks on Fifth Avenue, bring them home, and paint them I can swear to—for I made a small picture once of two gardenias against a black ground and I remember George Luks exclaiming loudly, "My god how beautiful—do some more—do some more." If I ever did I do not now remember. I only know I am always saying I will do some more—for it is the one white flower that really knows how to be white—how to look white and how to smell white. Only a year ago on the way up to Mexico from Vera Cruz there was a wondrous bush of gardenias at the foot of Orizaba, in the dark hands of the Mexicans, and I lived the gardenia over again—the perfect flower of all the white ones—the perfect white.

This I think will bring me up to the time of going to Paris.

Paris and Paradise

I went to Paris on *La Savoie*—and arrived duly at the Gare St. Lazare— most disappointed to find Paris was a dark city and was not made of "mother of pearl." For three days I stayed in a cheap tourist hotel to be near the Gare—too sort of bewildered to get myself away from that section. Three days after I got myself up to Montparnasse and found Lee Simonson eventually. It was all too hectic and brilliant, I thought—hundreds of artists—and so many faces that looked somehow famous to me. I learned whose they were later—they were Pascin, Zak, and Mme. Bosnanska—a little pale wondrous woman as if in the deepest of mourning always. "Why so black?" I said—the answer came—she is in mourning for Poland.[26]

Lee was going south to a place I had then never heard of—Cassis—to paint landscape and I think to join Macdonald-Wright who had a home there.[27] Lee had a real studio in a lovely street in back in a lovely garden. "I want to rent my studio," said Lee, "why don't you take it?" I found I could and had a grand studio in Paris—the only studio I ever had. I have never since that time had a studio—and this was about 1912–13—I have never felt I needed a studio and most of my pictures have been done in any kind of room and often on two chairs—and I still work on two chairs—sitting on one—the other the easel.

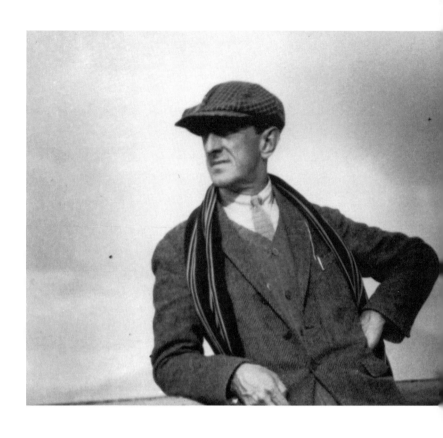

Hartley on board ship, "first trip abroad," 1912,
Marsden Hartley Collection, Yale Collection of
American Literature, Beinecke Rare Book and
Manuscript Library, Yale University.

There was a group of Americans at the Dôme then—presumably studying but playing billiards mostly.[28] I didn't feel at home at the Dôme—and used to have my coffee across the street at what is now the Rotonde, then just four tables at the corner outside—and a bistro inside—I ate my meals at Thomas' restaurant just around the corner. There I met Arnold Rönnebeck my first German friend, there I met Alice Miriam to whom he was engaged, there I met Charles Demuth.[29]

There was just one place left at Thomas' one evening and an American came up and asked if he could have it and we said "yes." Then he said something funny—and I said, "I guess you better come here all the time," and it has been like that ever since with Charles Demuth and me. It was still cold and we ate inside evenings at least. Then it got to be spring, summer, and autumn, and we ate outside on the terrace—and the sights are always fine on a Paris terrace because all the world goes by and you see it as you eat.

There was Zak and his mother every day—Zak so pale and dainty with a ring on his forefinger and a high black cane with an ivory head. There was Mme. Bosnanska mourning for Poland. Later there was a short handsome fellow in blue jeans with a woman and a big white dog—and they said it was Picasso, so of course I always looked hard when they passed. I learned then who Wilhelm Uhde was also. He was knowing Rousseau well just then.[30]

27 rue de Fleurus

That's a number and a street a lot of us remember.[31] I had of course heard of that number and the name Gertrude Stein, for I think Stieglitz had already published "One, One, One" in "Camera Work," being her portrait of Picasso. I remember a fine woman, Mrs. Charles Knoblauch, coming to 291 with a huge package of manuscripts, asking if Stieglitz would look at it and be interested. She didn't know what to make of it, but, "Here it is. Gertrude has sent them to me."

There were the Saturday evenings at 27 rue de Fleurus and was it perhaps Lee Simonson who took me there before he went south—I do not recall—but I was taken and Gertrude Stein was very nice to me—and

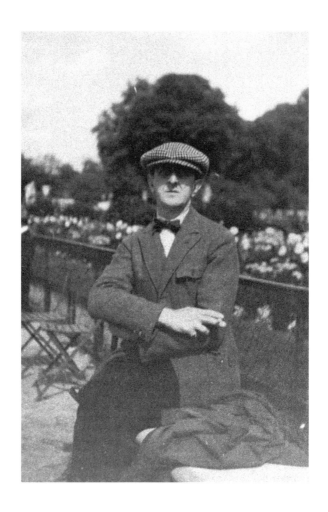

Hartley in the Luxembourg Gardens, Paris,
ca. 1912, Marsden Hartley Memorial Collection,
Museum of Art, Bates College.

Alice Toklas was very nice to me—and I seem to feel I was liked. I had to get used to so much of everything all at once of course—a room full of staggering pictures—a room full of strangers and two very remarkable looking women—Alice and Gertrude. I went often I think after that on Saturday evenings—still always thinking, in my reserved New England tone, "How do people do things like that—let everybody in off the street to look at their pictures?" But it seemed to be very à la mode then—and anyone or most anyone who had pictures would let anyone in to see them. So one got to see a vast array of astounding pictures—all burning with life and new ideas—and as strange as the ideas seemed to be—all of them terrifically stimulating—a new kind of words for an old theme. If I had known then what Emily Dickinson said about poetry I could have said the same thing about the paintings: "When I feel as if the top of my head would come off I know that is poetry—is there any other way?" I didn't know amazing Emily then—but that was what the pictures did to me— they seemed to burn my head off. I felt indeed sort of like a severed head living of itself by mystical excitation. But I knew it was all the best of art and must be looked at—and thought about—and that is always the best way about anything.

I started to work in the studio at 18 rue Moulin de Beurre. What a location to live in—such a wealth of life up the rue de la Gaîté and Ver-cingétorix—full of *apaches* then of course and many men with wide velve-teen trousers and sashes and capes—and their women in black shawls and remarkable coiffures—a bun at the back and a roll or bun at each temple and no hats. The rue de la Gaîté was full of them every Saturday evening, chiefly where they came to eat oysters—and drink white wine.

Alice Miriam was studying then with de Reszke—Jean I suppose— and lived way up beyond the Lion de Belfast—and didn't come to Thomas' often as she was paying de Reszke ten dollars a half hour and had to cook her own meals over the fireplace—six flights up—and that was a hard life for a singer.[32] She was unhappy about her work and felt her voice was getting worse and worse and was worried. So we didn't see her much at Thomas'—but she used to come by now and then and eat with us—

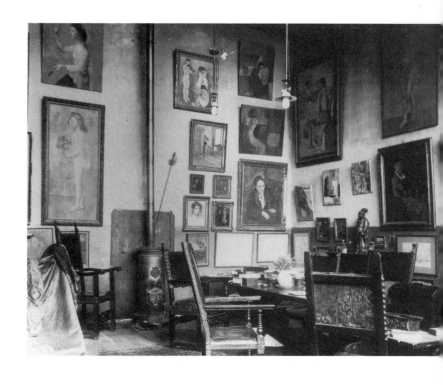

The atelier at 27 rue de Fleurus, ca. 1912,
Gertrude Stein Collection, Yale Collection of
American Literature, Beinecke Rare Book and
Manuscript Library, Yale University. Picasso's
famous 1907 portrait of Gertrude Stein is
prominently displayed in the center of the photo.

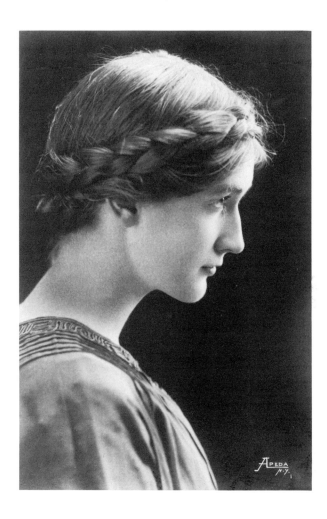

Alice Miriam Pinch, ca. 1919, courtesy of Michael
McMahon, Madison, Connecticut.

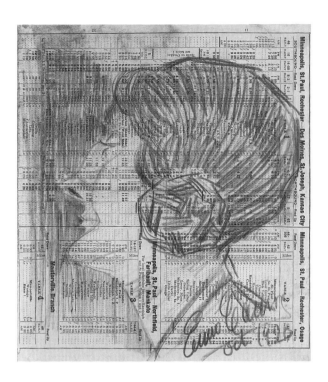

Enrico Caruso, sketch of Alice Miriam Pinch on a
train schedule, October 1920, courtesy of Michael
McMahon, Madison, Connecticut.

and rarely spend an evening with Arnold and me—and we were most happy together.

Alice went to Milan finally in the war, and found there an unknown music teacher by the name of Cunelli who opened her voice and she sang like a bird—and in Milan was taken by Gatti-Casazza to the Metropolitan later—she sang Micaëla in "Carmen" with Geraldine Farrar who loved her and was good to her.[33] Then quickly she got the chief role in "The Snow Maiden," but by that time—then that time her strength was going.[34] She had suffered too much hardship in the study period. She made a triumphal success in this role—and died. But she did get to the Metropolitan and that is what she so much wanted.

The death of Alice affected us all dreadfully for we had all gone through things together and it was our pride that Alice had come to her own and was getting recognition and engagements from all sides. She had a good voice and had learned how to use it—and when I saw her coming down over the rocks in Carmen—and heard her voice ring out of the great void—I shook all over for I had never really heard her sing. Then she was giving out the air of Micaëla with splendid vocalism and surety—there she is—Alice—our Alice—the Alice of all of us—the same little Alice we all knew so well in private life, with her corn coloured hair braided around her head, her pink complexion, her wise, witty naughty eye—and her so slim almost boyish figure. "I am a little boy," she said to me more than once, "some day I will show you." And one evening in 59th Street we were having lamb chops together—she in her kimono, staying home that evening. "I don't have to go to school tonight," meaning the Met Op school—as she used to have to do almost every night—to have her roles in readiness. Many times I would take her to the 60th Street subway—and one special night she said, "I must go and eat an apple in 'Louise.' That's what we girls have to do in opera." The one night she stayed at home—and we were talking about all kinds of things—suddenly she said with her honest and almost naughty boy eye, "I have told you so often I am a little boy." She stood up and opened her kimono and there I saw the image of youth—a radiant image, and I never saw her again.

We were extremely congenial, Alice and Arnold and I—and it was all set by Alice that when they married, and that too was set—whoever was successful first—they would marry. Alice said, "We will take an apartment and you will come to live with us"—and it so seemed it could be like that—for we all loved each other—we all had work to do and we all were interested in each other's progress. It was not to be.

But we are getting to 27 rue de Fleurus—the amazing room. Anyone knowing that room will come upon it in the intensest degree in the auto-biography of Alice Toklas—so vivid indeed that it seems strange that one is not physically there as one reads. It is without doubt the best portrait of a room that has been done by any of the moderns. It is a most speaking likeness. It is the room around Alice and Gertrude—it is them in the room it is the room with everybody passing through it and some of us remaining in it in whatever degree we could remain.

I was not then and I am not now the type of person who gets into a room easily. I always have to work my way in. I can be easy in a room when I have had time to get into it. I have to get settled—and see one thing at a time after I see all of it at once. That is no small job in a room like 27 rue de Fleurus—with walls all afire with epoch making ideas and at least two vivid people under them. I couldn't have entertained this room any too remarkably save that it has always had space and place for all sorts and kinds of things and qualities—for Gertrude has always had a way of liking several kinds of people at once. If they entertained her with smart talk or gossip all well and good and if they became something more homelike, more carpet slipperish, that was all right too. Maybe Gertrude lived by disembodiedness, which she says is so American. Surely I was one of that kind then—for I had a tendency toward extasy and exaltation then—and I think that must have made me likable. In any event I was happy I was liked. I shall go on now and tell something that maybe Gertrude will be annoyed at—but it is a part of the picture—something she said and meant then though she wouldn't and couldn't mean it now.

It was one of her Saturday nights and I was there—I recognized Delau-nay and Mme D.—having already presented a letter to them at their apart-ment from the late Samuel Halpert who knew many of the well-known people during his Paris days—including Rousseau—and spoke of a good French.[35] The room was full of strangers, probably the Hungarians Gertrude speaks of.[36] I was floundering about in my usual way in a busy room—Mme. Delaunay could speak English—and presently Delaunay turned to me and I at least understood him, "What kind of pictures do you paint?" and in typical American English style but in halting French, I said, "O I don't know." "What? You don't know? You don't know? A man paints and he doesn't know what he paints?" I was nervous by that time—and I called to Gertrude and said, "Tell this man to go to. . . ." "O I can't quite do that," she said—and laughed the usual rich laughter—and then she said, "But by the way, what *do* you paint?" It was much easier to say to her because she is my country woman—"O I don't know"—and she at once said, "I'd like to see." "O," I said, "that's nice—but you have seen hundreds of bad American paintings and I wouldn't want to bore you." And she said, "O no, may I come?" "Of course—but I warn you beforehand—don't expect anything"—and we made a date for the week following at my place for tea. I think Delaunay must have understood because he wanted to come to tea also. Gertrude said, "I want to see them first—I know Delaunay." I only tell this because what followed was a great satisfaction to me and did more for me than anything else could have done.

I had stopped doing beans and apples—and thought I would just take some canvases and begin more or less in the style of automatic writing and let my hand be guided as it were. I made lines and curves, stars and various images, and coloured them lightly so that the whole effect was to have an inspirational and transcendent quality. I found after I had done one, I could do more, and they began to be sort of portraits of moments. They were of good size, about thirty by forty inches, and I did at least twenty of them.

On the given day Gertrude and Alice came to Simonson's studio and I had arranged the pictures around the floor in a row and on chairs and easels—and the tea table to one side—and I had made sandwiches of fine whole wheat bread, *petit suisse*, and finely chopped endives—which I had never heard of, but found they tasted good—and they were liked and commented on. And it was time to look at the pictures—and Gertrude's comment was, "Well, Hartley, I wasn't expecting anything like this—I really like them—at last an original American." Pardon Gertrude—you said it then—you wouldn't say it now maybe—but I thought it nice to hear all the same. I had started off to explore some other space and I seemed to have set something down—and the more I did of them the more authentic they looked. An American journalist and his occultist wife came to see them and she said, "You have no idea what you are doing—these pictures are full of Kabbalistic signs and symbols"—and I felt taken down—for I had no intention or hope of being profound. It upset me.

Gertrude said finally, "I want to come again and see these pictures—so I can see how I feel about them after I have gone." So we set the same day the following week. Then it was I think that Delaunay wanted to come with Bruce and it was suggested that Apollinaire might also come.[37] But none of them came, just Alice and Gertrude—and there was more tea and more of the same sandwiches—and Gertrude said she hadn't changed her mind about the pictures—and that she liked them—then suggested I go to their place one day to lunch, bring some of the pictures and take down some of the Matisses and Picassos and stick them in their places. "You will see they will hold their own," said Gertrude—and it was naturally a most edifying experience for me—and helped me greatly then.

These same pictures went later to Munich and were shown by the *Blaue Reiter* group of which Marc, Kandinsky, Klee, et al. were the leaders.

If I am recalling rightly it was that first Christmas in Paris I went to Berlin to visit the family of Rönnebeck and Berlin for the first time. I was so overcome with the speed, the brilliance, the spotlessness of the life and the city that I moved there later—bringing forth a typical Gertrude portrait "A cook can see—pointedly in uniform."[38] On the way back I was certain it was then—I went by way of Munich, saw an exhibition of Franz Marc at the Tannhauser Gallery, liked it, and from Paris wrote to Marc in English that I had enjoyed it and what I thought it had in it. And there was some correspondence in English and French—ending then with the invitation to exhibit with this group. I thanked Marc in the next letter and said, "You are all very kind but you have not seen the pictures." "That's all right—we like the way you talk," he replied, and the pictures went on to Munich. I followed them and there was a typical fest made of the event—Kandinsky, Klee, Campendonk, Münter, Werefkin, Marc and Frau Marc, Bechtejeff—all came in from their mountain villages and made a day of it.[39] They said they didn't understand the pictures but liked them, and arranged for a show of them in a new gallery in the Prauner Strasse which I couldn't wait to see. I am sure I went back to Paris to pack up and go to Berlin to live, as I was so impressed with all that flair and perfection of the Kaiser regime. "Many bright soldiers and peaceable in the rest of the stretch" was I think the last line of the portrait "A cook can see."[40] I had had a rich experience in the room at 27 rue de Fleurus. I had taken Rönnebeck there whom Alice and Gertrude liked. Arnold has a wondrous gift for languages, speaks English almost perfectly, French so flawlessly they wouldn't believe he was German, and could write almost without error in English and of course in French.

I had seen the lovely face of Kahnweiler making a fine portrait through the doorway of his little office in back, at the rue Vignon—something like a Bronzino boy in a way.[41] I had been often there to see the Picassos and the Braques which then were so alike in treatment it was difficult for a new eye to know whose. Kahnweiler's face is still fine—but there is something different now. Many things happened to him in the next years. I still think it wonderful that men like him and Uhde went back after all that had happened to them but they are both inviolable lovers of France and both of them peacefully living on as if nothing had happened. Uhde is now dealing in and with the waifs in painting—the famous *concierge* Séraphine—and all the others—has a house full of them in his place at Chantilly.[42] Nice person, Uhde—so sensitive, so cultivated, so friendly, and so touchingly unforgetting. Years after all this he remembered me and asked me to Chantilly.

And so I had been initiated in the new arts of Paris—and I was I felt certain more intelligent than I had ever been—for none of these arts were foreign to me at the first moment. They were all so alive and pulsing I accepted all of them from the first.

I moved the following May 1914 to Berlin. My visit then was to the Rönnebeck family who were so friendly and so kind and to this day nearly twenty years are still among my best friends. The intense flamelike quality of the life there—for things were of course up on their toes and ready to kick off. Such spick and spanness in the order of life I had never witnessed anywhere—not merely because the military life provided the key and clue to everything then—but this sense of order flowed over into common life—and such cleanliness prevailed as hardly to believe—the pavements shining like enamel leather. I recall being much impressed with the cream white taxis lined with red leather—so much so that when Rönnebeck put me into one—I remember thinking—no professors' sons have cars as elegant as this. I soon saw of course that there were dozens of others of the same grandeur.

I had never felt such a sense of voluptuous tension in the air anywhere. It was all so warm to my long chilled New England nature and provided the sense of home always so needed in my life and which Germans so often tendered long before I found the way to go to Europe. It was Germans— German Jewish friends who offered me home, friendliness, hospitality, bread, life, belief. It was they who fed me out of their hearts, they who saw and believed in what they saw, they who have been doing it all my life— and with one or two exceptions the only ones who have consistently believed and put their belief into operation.

As I say the air of Berlin was tense with vitality and a most human quality—probably all told one of the ugliest cities of the world—probably all told one of the most genial—most companionable. A week in Berlin made me feel that one had come home—and it is easy to see what four years of constant living there has done. I always feel I am coming home when I get into Germany, quite as I used to feel when I crossed the line of the State of Maine at South Berwick—I always knew I was in New England. Coming to Berlin then had quite the same effect on me—and of course I soon began to have friends, chiefly Rönnebeck's friends—who took me in and liked me.

There was so much to regale the eye with—that is, the new-learning eye—all to be a vividly revealing aspect of enlarging experience. Rönnebeck knew of my love for any kind of pageantry, all coming from early boyhood and the big days of the year, the coming of the circus to Lewiston—the real Barnum's circus, and the annual State Fair—and remaining forever more a living issue in my life. Rönnebeck knew this and so began to initiate me into German style. Of course in the Kaiser time there was always a parade of some kind coming down the Unter den Linden—just as now in the Hitler time there is always a parade coming from somewhere, for vastly different reasons each time because each Germany was vastly different.

So of course there was always the changing of the watch before the castle in Berlin every morning between ten thirty and eleven—and a concert after of fine music excellently played—for all Germans are innately musical. I had arrived in Berlin at the right time to get the richness of the pageantry idea. There was still the sense of magic in seeing royalty pass—and that you could do at any home in Berlin then—for the family was always either coming from or going to Potsdam.

It was not long before there was to be a stupendous festival. I think I must by then have seen the spring parade for the Kaiser at the Tempelhofer Feld—and a huge event was to take place for the daughter of the Kaiser was to be married to the Herzog von Braunschweig, and all the living royalties of Europe were present. It was of course the age of iron—of blood and iron, every back bone in Germany was made of it—or had new iron poured into it—the whole scene was fairly bursting with organized energy and the tension was terrific and somehow most voluptuous in the feeling of power—a sexual immensity even in it—when passion rises to the full and something must happen to quiet it.

All this was very exciting—appealing—and novel to the little boy on the second step in the Tapley photo, and the same little boy likes all these things still and will like them to the end—for it is countless people and their energy all in one place—that makes him feel alive. As most or as many people are inclined to shudder at the mention of the word "crowd"—

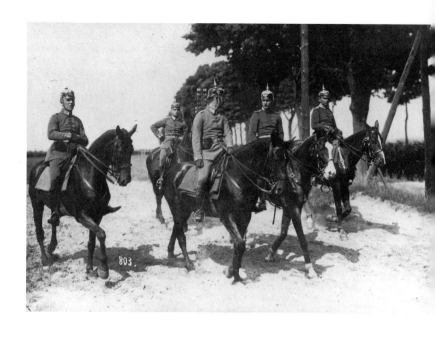

Prussian soldiers, unautographed postcard
photograph, Marsden Hartley Collection, Yale
Collection of American Literature, Beinecke Rare
Book and Manuscript Library, Yale University.

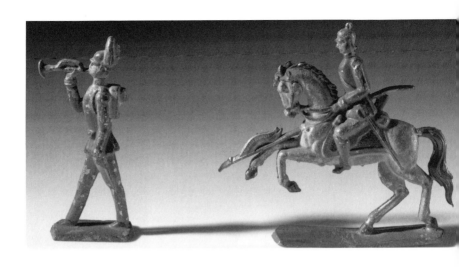

Toy Prussian soldiers, Marsden Hartley Memorial
Collection, Museum of Art, Bates College, photo by
Melville McLean. Hartley was a collector of
mementos and souvenirs. These figurines, obviously
not from his childhood but acquired during World
War I or later, probably reminded him of his
friendships in Berlin in 1914–15.

it had quite the contrary effect upon me than upon most of quieting me and making me feel at home. I could always know that I was quite like other people when I was with a lot of people. It would take me out and make me feel outward and that has always been necessary—for it is a very bad thing to live inside so much—as no one has learned better than myself. So at last I could have all I wanted of crowd parade pageantry public glamour—and the like.

The morning came for the entry through the Brandenburger Tor of the Hohenzollen princess and her duke to be—the Pariser Platz was packed jammed to the stoops and windows with those huge cuirassiers of the Kaiser's special guard—all in white—white leather breeches skin tight—high plain enamel boots—those gleaming blinding medieval breast plates of silver and brass—making the eye go black when the sun glanced like a spear as the bodies moved. There were the inspiring helmets with the imperial eagle and the white manes hanging down—there was six foot of youth under all this garniture—everyone on a horse—and every horse white— that is how I got it—and it went into an abstract picture of soldiers riding into the sun, a fact to take place not so long after—for all of these went out into the sun and never came back.

In the procession was of course every royalty then known to Europe. I see the faces of the Tzar and Tzarina of Russia—the ill-fated Romanoffs who came to a terrible end. There were King George and Queen Mary— and was the Prince of Wales there also? I seem to think he was. It was the biggest display of pageantry I had or have ever seen—it was the Hohenzollen princess being crowned Herzogin von Braunschweig. It was all glamour and stimulus for the boy inside—and the boy was at least thirty-five by then—and how thick and fast life had come all at once—the huge year in Paris—with the revelations of the Louvre and the new modern masters. The coming face to face with so much life and art all at once—was all but blinding—but I have blue eyes and blue eyes can take in all things and not be disturbed by them—except to be extatically disturbed—which is their way of being passionate.

I was once stopped in the public gardens of Boston, in that Boston period of which I have spoken, by a man whom I thought to be a beggar—

and as poor as I myself then was, I was reaching for a five cent piece mechanically for the usual cup of coffee that is asked for. The man was poorly clothed but he was not begging. All he said was, "Excuse me—may I look into your eyes? Please understand me—I am an unhappy man—I am not begging—it does me good to look into your blue eyes." I seemed to know what pain was and I understand this—because I had had all kinds of strange experiences then—many unpleasant ones because I have only one way of looking and that is straight, and I have been roughly accosted more than once for past looking—because many people in trouble do not like to be looked at so directly. But this was a human experience and I understood it. Soon his eyes began to moisten and rain—and then there was a flow of Catholic images coming from his thoughts—one of which was, "Your eyes are like the blue robe of the Virgin Mary"—this is fact and not fiction I am telling. I know now I should have said, "Go to Mary, she can help you more"—but all I said was, "I understand—and if it helps you to look—just do it"—and the tense moment passed and the man quietly thanked me for understanding and went on his way. I myself was straining subconsciously toward heaven in that period and I suppose my eyes had something in them that came out. I have always wondered what brown eyes see because my eyes have always been of the bluest blue. And so my eyes were experiencing all they could manage then of splendour of pageantry and it seemed to fill the longing of endless years of hunger—and so I was very busy every day looking and looking.

I settled down readily into the life of Berlin—for I had good friends who were being very kind to me. I was hearing the best music—and, as I was caring more then for the theatre, I was seeing all the novelties of these new ideas of the theatre: five hours of Wagner in one form, and four or five hours of two parts of "Faust" "on wheels" done by Reinhardt, who had then introduced the revolving stage, and all the famous new lighting—dome ceilings and all that—which was to reveal so much to a man like Robert Edmond Jones who had come to Berlin for his theatrical education and was sent to me with a letter from Mabel Dodge.[43] Jones was I think the first to come from America for this purpose—and the best theatres were opened to him from front to back through the kindness of the producer of the Reinhardt theatres—the Volksbühne and the Charlottenburg Opernhaus—all the great new wonders of the theatre world then.

Jones went home eventually to New York and began to show Broadway a different world and of course found his solid place then at once. From a life of hardship—he flowed into another life of success—not however without new struggles I fancy, for the New York theatres had to be made all over to compete with the European ideas.

Not long after this—being May—a new theatre decided to give its first performance, and in August 1914 the entire world was let in upon what it now knows too well—and from which it will take centuries to recover. It had of course its glamour to the observer —and it was all so fantastic that none of it seemed real. I remember a girl friend of then, an American, and myself talking like two infants, saying, "O it will probably be all over by Christmas and we will be among the first outsiders who have seen it."

October came—and it took one of my most cherished friends and all that went with him—out into the great drama, in August—for it swept all the first ones off like wheat flattened to the ground by lightening and thunder.[44] The sense had then come of what it was all about and what was to follow. No use going into all of this because everyone knows the rest and tragic novels are still being written of it—for it was a great story— and alas so terribly and so tragically inhuman.

The end of 1915 came—and everybody was some time before this receiving bread only by card—and only so much in the week. Most of us by then after much difficulty had come to the end of our means and were obliged to go home—I not able to believe that America would soon be coming in, and I would have found myself a guest at Ruheleben—a not very enticing name inasmuch as it was already meaning quite the reverse to Englishmen and others of the opposing countries, and so I went to Holland and took the boat home from there to New York.[45]

The next aspect of life was Mabel Dodge's salon. I am sure I must have met Mabel at Gertrude's as Rönnebeck also did—for Mabel had asked us to be her guests later in the summer at the Villa Curonia. We were to have gone—I had my trunk already for the romantic episode—then a telegram came from Florence from Mabel saying not to come, as she would have to be leaving and so we never got to see and know the famous Villa Curonia—Carl Van Vechten, Bobby Jones, and others being already there. So I found Mabel in New York—and that was what could be called "a winter."[46]

Mabel had furnished her apartment with remarkable Italian furnishings and had brought several of her Italian servants with her—and it was all like a jewel-box pouring out shafts of amazing light—at least for my always amorous blue eyes. The house was always full of people and I got to know them all. Mabel had asked me to dinner—and then she had bought a picture called "Rapture" from me which I had for years always wanted to do over, as I had learned the meaning of the word better after that—but it was an attempt at a portrait of a word. It was later transferred to Taos, New Mexico—had changed hands, and was found in a shed or a store room there and bought by Paul Strand—to rescue it I am sure.

Mabel liked me, and I liked her and all the entourage for they were all vivid—full of life. There was to begin with the now so known and loved John Reed of Oregon who was at that time being a most successful war correspondent and if I recall rightly was then back from Mexico and had interviewed Pancho Villa—and had published his story.[47]

Mabel said, "Come any time—don't wait to be asked—come to lunch—to dinner—come in and sit down—rest—write—read—be at home"—and we were all wonderfully together there. A certain group always there—all day and all evening sometimes.

Jack Reed was a wonderful human being as everyone knows. He had great fire and an intense interest in everything human. He was interesting himself then in the Paterson strikes—and staged some kind of a huge pageant in Madison Square—the meaning of which I never did know for I didn't know people for their ideas—any more than I do now.[48] I knew them just for themselves—and painters and poets never thought of things of action I fear at that time.

But there was constant movement at Mabel's for she liked life and had always drawn it and as she seldom or never went out—that is, evenings to opera or theater—she had life pour into her house—and pour it did—

and fullness poured with it. Wednesday was the special evening and someone came and expounded something, or read something, and there was a
huge feast of food afterward—the largest turkey, the largest ham, the
largest bowl of grapefruit salad, stacks of bread. The buffet was lined with
bottles—numbers to the hundreds came in and ate—many of whom were
unknown to the hostess or to us regular guests. You looked and saw all the
strange faces of the world under the flare of a crystal chandelier. Some of
us became friends of years—such as Andrew Dasburg, and you will get
quite something of all that from Carl Van Vechten's book—is it not all in
"Peter Whiffle"?[49]

The winter ended—a bit too theatrically I seem to recall, for Bill
Haywood had come to talk and the next day the papers were full of the
"Big Sweep" or the exact headline was "Society Matron Entertains Anar-
chists," etc.[50]

The summer found a lot of us at Provincetown—surely the biggest
summer that most of us have lived through. Jack Reed, being as I say a
most successful journalist and war correspondent, had taken a good sized
house for the summer and had invited several of us to be his summer guests.

The Provincetown Players began their work that summer in the little
fish house of Mary Heaten Vorse—and it was made into a theater.[51] Susan
Glaspell and her husband George Cram Cook were the leading spirits in
this movement and the star playwright was to be Eugene O'Neill and several of Gene's short plays were done that summer.[52] Gene lived in a fisher's
hut across the way—and the Cooks in a lovely little white house which
was their home. The Hapgoods, Neith and Hutchins, were "down along,"
Mary H. V. across from them.[53] Charles Demuth was a guest there that
summer—Max Eastman, Ida Rauh.[54] Mabel had a house at the far end of
the street out of things—Leo Stein was one of her guests I think—and
the best of a good time was had by all—for we were all congenial in our
various ways.

George Cook or "Jig," as everyone called him, was an indefatigable
worker in his little theatre idea and worked day and night for it—did
probably all the carpenter work besides—everybody that was interested
acted, sewed, or worked somehow for this theatre—and it got to be an

absolutely real thing—and when winter came it was taken to McDougal Street and everyone knows the rest of that story.[55]

Was it then about—that the Russian development was taking place—and Jack Reed either went on his own or was sent—and Louise Bryant another journalist went with him. I know nothing of all this save that Jack and Louise were in full swing in the Russian movement—Jack somehow or other becoming more and more a figure in it—and must somehow or other have meant a great deal to the Russians at that time.

There was an epidemic of typhus then also. Jack was taken desperately ill—and from the big fine wholesome thing that he was, wasted to nothing and died—was given a full military funeral and buried in the Kremlin—quite something out of Jack's line I am certain for he was not out for heroics—he was just being human as always. We all felt the loss of Jack terrifically for he belonged to all of us.

Cook after several years of struggle with the Provincetown Players was sort of tired I guess, and satisfied a life long wish—by going to Greece. He had I think taught Greek in a small midwestern university.[56] Mrs. Cook or Susan Glaspell went with him—and there was unfolded one of the most singular transformations—for Cook had become a real Greek. He grew a long beard, adopted the Greek shepherd's costume, roamed the hills with the shepherds, and told them Greek stories in their own language that they had never heard. He also took sick of some insular disease and died several days after—received recognition from the Greek government—was buried near the temple of Delphi—and a stone from the temple was placed above him.

Could anything have been more like the fulfillment of a boy's dream than this—and you get all this from Susan Glaspell's remarkable portrait of Cook called I think the "Road to the Temple"—which is by way of being I always thought—a perfect portrait of Susan herself.[57] I was always fond of Susan and still am—I liked her New Englandism—for she had come back to her own earth from the middle west where she was born—and where her family had migrated.

I had heard that Susan had arrived from Greece after the death of Cook—and was staying with friends. I asked if it was thought that Susan would care to see me or anyone so soon after her return—and the answer was, "O yes—she would like to see you." So I spent the evening with her alone and her recital of the Greek episode was one of the most poetical things I had ever heard spoken—for Susan always spoke poetry—her plainest phrases were nearly always ready-written ones—they were always a little too good for the theatre into which she had ventured.

What a summer—in among those amazing dunes—shifting with the wind before one's eyes—burying young pine trees to their tops—moving incessantly, statistics said at the rate of several inches a year. Whoever will forget those dunes—once having seen them—and the great rumbling, dramatic "outside" as it was called—the ocean itself, the long stretch of lonely sands, and nothing else but the life saving station—which if I recall rightly was to be the home of Gene O'Neill for several succeeding years, where he went on writing his now so well known plays and from which I think he afterwards shifted to Bermuda—or was it Bermuda after the Ridgewood, Connecticut, period? In any event the house in Bermuda is now known as the Eugene O'Neill house—and Bermuda prides itself therewith. We all went back of course to New York—and I seem to recall nothing much except my usual exhibitions in the Stieglitz group—until the next period which was to be New Mexico and Taos.

A rich woman I had come to know was going out there and wanted a teacher—and encouraged me to go there—later on she decided she wanted to paint by herself—and so compromised by buying a picture—a pastel I think it was. I was completely disappointed in Taos as a place and could never get myself to go back there—and when the epidemic of the flu swept the country and finally landed in Taos, I felt I must take the precaution as people were already beginning to die there—and I moved down to Sante Fe which I liked much better—and was kindly received there.

It was that summer that Mabel had begun buying houses and making them over—the large one for herself and the small ones all around her she eventually bought so that she might have only friends for neighbors. Later on the Lawrence period began—and you will have all that in "Lorenzo in Taos." [58]

I of course enjoyed the Indians and their dances and saw I think nearly all the Indian dances, both at Taos and those all round Sante Fe. The Indian was not so popular as he is now among the esthetes and it was not always so easy to see the dances—that is, you were let in if you were properly recommended. I wrote at that time a rapturous defense of the Indians and their dances which was published in "Art and Archaeology"—which seemed to be liked—chiefly by the archaeologists who were then fighting the government—for there was a movement on then to stop the dances.[59] This defense came out in a book called "Adventure in the Arts" with a preface by Waldo Frank.[60]

Besides the Indians, my chief memory of a human being was the remarkable figure of one Jack Bidwell who was living up in the mountains guarding the machinery of a defunct copper mine—at a dead mining village—called, is it not, Twinning?

That summer in Taos—besides Leo Stein—another guest of Mabel's was Elizabeth Duncan, whom I much enjoyed and whom I was later to see more often in the 1920 period in Berlin—for she had been given large quarters for her dancing school in the New Palace in Potsdam.[61]

Bidwell was a remarkable figure and looked like a piece of a mountain—he was huge in build—with a face like a militant crusader. He was an intense lonely thing as I see him standing in the doorway of one of those mining huts at Twinning facing the day and light such as only a hard man can face it.

The legend is a powerful one and there is no reason why it can't be told. In his youth he was a member of this mining community which then must have flourished considerably as the machinery of the mine was the most expensive imaginable and in an excellent state of preservation. The mine had gone broke and the village long since deserted—only another of those countless western mining tales.

Bidwell had killed a man in the name of social justice—one of the miners who had proved himself so thoroughly a social menace in this community. So great was the pressure against him—mass emotion driving terrifically against him—and from all accounts with justice—that the thought was projected—somebody must kill him—and Bidwell killed him. The whole community embraced him. The matter went to court, Bidwell was freed, and forever after was a miserable man, for he had killed someone against his own will. That is how the story came—and for many years Bidwell suffered the conscience of the guilty.

It was a cruel thing to see Bidwell facing the day—and no one who ever saw him forgets him I am certain.

Santa Fe was a charming city. It was full of nice people who had gone there for their health—recovered it—and settled. What it is now like I know only by hearsay—and it is now the rendezvous of the artists and the writers—and is most decidedly on the esthetic map at this hour. Perhaps it is just as nice as it was then—but I have no feeling for art colonies.

The end of that epoch came. I had done a few paintings of more or less significance—one of them was purchased by the museum—and I still hear every now and then of this picture.[62]

I was wanting to see California—and knew if I didn't go while I was out that way I would be hardly likely to later—and so it is—I have never been since.

I had made the acquaintance of Carl Sprinchorn of Swedish birth in Provincetown—a friendship which was to last out the years.[63] Sprinchorn had gone to Los Angeles on a tragic mission, to take the body of Rex Slinkard home—a very talented painter—who was doing military service in the East—was caught in the terrible flu epidemic and died. Slinkard was also a pupil of Henri and I am sure that Slinkard and Sprinchorn were the only real romanticists in that otherwise school of realism.[64]

I had never heard of Slinkard there—but I came to know him very well after he had died—for I went out to share a house with Sprinchorn at a place called La Cañada, then just beginning to be settled by tourists and is probably now completely so—if only that it is not far from Pasadena and Hollywood.

Carl talked to me a great deal of Rex. He wanted me to see his drawings and took me in to Los Angeles to meet Gladys Williams, the fiancee of Rex, a beautiful and most lovable person who was to fall heir to Rex's pictures and drawings. Gladys had learned mounting, as she did not want

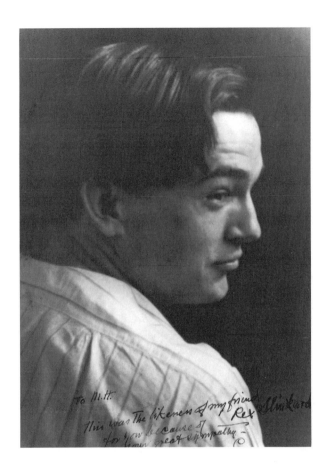

Rex Slinkard, photo signed to Marsden Hartley by
Carl Sprinchorn, Marsden Hartley Collection, Yale
Collection of American Literature, Beinecke Rare
Book and Manuscript Library, Yale University.

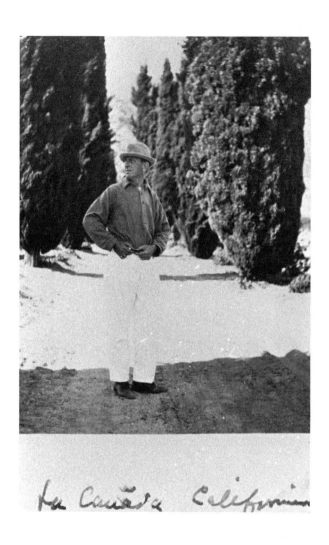

Hartley in La Cañada, California, 1918, Marsden
Hartley Collection, Yale Collection of American
Literature, Beinecke Rare Book and Manuscript
Library, Yale University.

strange hands to handle these drawings. The drawings she had at the house and the paintings were in storage. I was later taken to see them and wrote what came to be a preface for a catalog of a show of these drawings and paintings. The exhibition was splendidly given in a huge room—and later on the same show was put on in New York by Knoedler's, when Mrs. Marie Sterner was in charge of the upper room.[65]

"I can't understand," said Henri to me—when I met him at this show—"how it was you never knew Rex personally—it is a very remarkable portrait of him." All I said was "Things come to one sometimes if one is interested"—and of course the drawings and paintings were a perfect revelation of a person.

Rex had left New York and all that, being dissatisfied with his life and work there, and wanted to do something about his own California. So he returned home, went to work tending to the irrigation ditches on the family ranch, carved little stones with very Greeklike profiles, and painted Sundays in the basement of the house.

I wonder how much California is caring for one of its most talented sons and painters?

Gladys Williams wanted to present the entire collection to the State of California—the show was given again in San Francisco—but I have never heard that the State made acceptance of this proffered gift. Later Gladys was to die herself at Banning and a delicate romance was sealed. I do not remember how much longer Sprinchorn stayed on in California—several months surely—and I was to come back again to New York.

I had met through Kreymborg a lady in Los Angeles who was the spirit of a poetry society there. She asked me if I would read some American poetry at one of her afternoons. I remember I had chosen, among many others, Carlos Williams, and Wallace Gould—who was a native of my Lewiston and whom I had met there during the winter of teaching and whom I was to know for years afterward, and who was to be introduced through me to Kreymborg, Williams, Rosenfeld, and others—through his poetry, and later to meet and know some of them personally.[66] After hard years of playing the piano in a movie house—the old "Music Hall" of my cousin—he had found the way to go south. I also said to the poetry lady, "I have read some aviation poems of a poet by the name of Robert McAlmon," and she replied, "He lives here in Los Angeles and will be here this afternoon." [67]

McAlmon and I became friends and I saw a lot of him there—and when I decided to go east, said he was going east too, to try his fortunes. In a short time he was there—and landed one morning—came to see me early and at nine o'clock said he was going to look for a job. At ten had found one with Egmont Arens and the Washington Square Book Shop. So much for western energy and faith.

He met Williams and many others—and soon he began to get letters from an English girl who was seeing America with H. D., the American poet.[68] They returned to New York en route for London. Bryher took a fancy to McAlmon for himself apparently, and in no time they were married and sailed for London all shivers, as McAlmon said, for he didn't know how he would be received in the English home. But Sir John Ellerman and Lady Ellerman took a fancy to him—and everything was all right. They liked his freshness and his energy and soon McAlmon began to do what he wanted to do—to have carte blanche to print prose and poetry he believed in—and became one of those "live wires" in Paris. He connected with Darantière the printer there at Dijon and printed the writings of a number of people and was later to print "The Making of Americans"— the thousand page story.[69]

Gertrude tells all this in her autobiography of Alice Toklas—and other revealing episodes in her experience—especially the French and American ones.

Then Came the Auction

I can only tell of outstanding events in this story to the little boy in the photo.

Then Came the Auction.

It was another period of pressure, and what painter does not experience them? I had gone that morning heavy with depression to see Stieglitz and said, "I can't stand the idea of that storage being a millstone around my neck—ten years now and those pictures in the dark and nobody wants them. I see no other way than to take them out and burn them."

Stieglitz, who always knew the struggles of his protégés, said, "I have been thinking about all that. Kennerley and I have been talking this over and we think it would be a fine idea to have an auction here in the Anderson Galleries if it is agreeable to you." [70] "Anything is agreeable to me that lets me live if I am to live," I said. The plan was laid before me. They had worked it all out—two weeks nearly of exhibition. The pictures were brought out of storage—in due time placed on the walls and there were 117 of them. The idea was of course spectacular—I do not know whether it was Kennerley's—or Stieglitz's—save that Kennerley, being director at that time of the Anderson Galleries, knew all about auctions and Kennerley was always very kindly disposed toward me and my work and was forever a solid friend of Stieglitz—believed in him—and I think even asked him to come into the Anderson Building and take number 303. The room that was to be the successor of 291—and continued its work in another style.

In any event the auction was a novel affair. It had never been done before with modern pictures. The pictures were put on the wall of two or was it three good size rooms—and the remainder were strung about in an outer hall. My feeling about it all is that it was a bit of vaudeville as regards myself, for there was everything I had ever tried to do and a lot of them not successes, but they were the work at least of one being more or less intelligent—and wanting in the end to be a good picture maker of some sort. Everybody came to the exhibition—hundreds and hundreds during the almost two weeks and the thing was announced, that is, the sale, for a certain date. I fancy a lot of people were intrigued with the idea of a bargain, as they are at any auction sale—for it makes no difference what it is—the household effects of a beauty or the last relics of a down and out. Auctions are auctions—and they are usually the auctions of belongings of people in straightened circumstances, for which title I was and have often been signified—and which title I hold perfectly today.

The auction day was getting nearer and nearer and I was getting more hectic with it—because I felt it could so easily be a failure—and I wasn't prepared to support a failure.

The day itself came—the pictures came down. Then it was time for the auction in the evening. Cars of all kinds were driving up. There was a little tone of theatre or opera about it—and I was bewildered. I had coffee that evening with Alice Miriam and her sister across the street in 59th Street—and as they were all going I thought perhaps I could slide in with them. Arriving at the door I proceeded to have a few more nerves than usual because I saw the room was packed to the doors—the auctioneer was at the stand—the lights were duly set.

Finally I thought I might get myself in at the back someplace—and as the show had begun I was able to do this without being noticed by many. The novelty was so marked that I completely forgot that it was all about me—and didn't even become conscious of the prices—save that some of them went for ten dollars, I remember.

As at all auctions there were certain pictures that many seemed to want and the bidding was keen. Dr. Albert Barnes bought two to his liking and put them in his foundation museum—and has thought them good enough to keep. Not long ago he said to me, "You'd be surprised how well they look," which was nice.[71]

I also remember Dr. William Carlos Williams was the purchaser of a pastel which he still has on his drawing room walls in his Rutherford, New Jersey, home, which home a lot of us knew well over a span of years.

The rapidity with which the performance took place astounded me— for I think it was all over before ten in the evening and had only begun at eight thirty or nine. The results next day were flattering in the extreme for a poor man—for the 117 netted me—3,900 dollars if I remember rightly—the remainder being taken up in the costs of staging and the usual incidents.

It was considered by everyone a triumph and still is talked of—nothing indeed like a novelty to amuse New York. I was safe and sound once more and could go on with the education of an artist. The storage was empty after ten years—and now it is full again—in the lapse of another ten.

There is one defect about the "art game" in New York: once a show is over—interest habitually ceases until the following year. As the Stieglitz gallery was not a commercial gallery and there was no storage room the pictures had to be carted away. A few were always kept of course—but there was never a dealer like a French dealer to take a chance on a painter— and keep him going by the principle of a year's business and not by the single exhibition. An exhibition generally produces two kinds of possible purchaser—the one who wants a private view all for himself—and the one who comes in after it is all over and wants them all hauled out again.

One of the chief supporters during the shows at 303 was a distinguished gentleman from Columbus, Ohio—Mr. Howald by name— whose interest in pictures was very genuine, and he seemed to like to be finding out things for himself.[72] Over a space of years he had, I have recently learned by the catalog of the new Columbus Museum of Art, given I think 100,000 dollars toward the building and presented his collection to it which was to be kept intact. It is the only museum in America that shows an American artist "en bloc," for better or worse—for Howald has gathered something like nearly thirty Marin water colours, twentysome Preston Dickinsons, a number of Charles Demuths, and sixteen oils of myself. The idea of course is very gratifying for besides supporting us—and we were all of us always struggling—it gave us recognition for whatever there was in us—and it curiously enough took me back to my beginnings in Cleveland where the museum now owns one of my New Mexican landscapes—of which I am in no sense ashamed—for I was there, three years ago and saw it on the walls then in company with Pissarro, Sisley, Monet, and, if I am not mistaken, Picasso and Matisse—and that is test enough for anyone—this picture being the purchase and gift of a young man who prefers to remain anonymous.

A passing reference here is applicable to a winter spent in Bermuda because several of the pictures sold in the auction were done there, chief among them being those purchased by Dr. Barnes. The winter in Bermuda was, to use a Jamesian turn of phrase, a handsome one—I had never seen such an array of sky-blue, pink, and chocolate homes and they were such a contrast to the little white snug ones of New England—the proverbial white with green blinds.

This was at the entire end of the war—the mines were still laid however and had not been taken up—and as people were not going down then—

chiefly from sea terror—there was almost no one there—all the large hotels of Hamilton were closed—and the old barracks of a hotel, the old St. George's, was compelled by law to remain open—and as they were glad to have any guests at all board was to be had surprisingly cheap.

Bermuda had immense charm then—I expect it always has—but it was quiet that winter—no one scarcely but the Bermudians themselves and the regiments from England sent over there during the war for light service. The whole flavour of the islands was of course very English—and you didn't have to hunt for it then as a I fancy one does now since the tourist trade has been reestablished. But Bermuda is itself and will never change—a little bijoux of a place, a glorious place for sunbathing where for once at the military beach we could lie about in the sun with nothing on and be undisturbed and that was my daily routine every morning all winter—sunning at the beach, painting—when it could be done—and listening to the two oldish ladies of the late Victorian regime gossip about the past—the meeting of English army and navy men and their wives—and a quiet peaceful time. Demuth came down to join me that winter and liked to talk of his thrills of that period.

The auction was over—there was bread in the basket for two years—and it was spring and the next move was to Paris again.

The summer in Paris was gay and amusing—there is always one summer in Paris when it is that.

There had been some sort of disagreement with Monsieur Jambon [?] of the Dôme—and the entire crew of artists and poets and whatnot shifted itself over to the Rotonde. The entire summer was spent on the terrace of the Rotonde and it was a gay summer—and everybody who came to Paris came to the Rotonde. It was my one conspicuous experience as a cafe-hound. There were of course many Americans and we all knew each other well—and there was Foujita of before the fame with his then lady—and a Japanese friend always present—if you saw any you saw the three or two waiting for one.[73] There is never a time of course when Paris is not enjoyable. It is probably the only city in the world that doesn't have a season—I don't mean in the high society sense—but in the common sense. You don't leave Paris in the summer because whatever heat there may be is either agreeable or endurable. And you meet the world there of course—and it is always fun to do that once.

I don't recall any one special thing of that summer—save that the season was harmonious and everybody enjoyed everybody else. It would take too long to go into names—but there were plenty with names—that is names in the making then, like Edna St. Vincent Millay, Robert McAlmon, Foujita, Djuna Barnes—and others. The autumn came—and I had already made plans for Berlin. Sometime before I went I was thought of as the artist who had inherited a fortune at that time—and by the end of the season the inheritance had grown to fifty thousand dollars, and I was on the list apparently of the poor and the helpless. I had to explain the myth away more than once.

I had probably spoken of going to Berlin to McAlmon at least—so that by the time I got going myself a little bevy of boys and girls had all got themselves up there and were to become millionaires of the inflation. Only yesterday here in Bavaria a native said to me, "We were all millionaires then." It was fantastic, this sinking of the mark, and I never did recall to how many billions of marks to the dollar it went—but it was fantastic.

That was the period of the Second Reich and its first as a republic—and the conditions were already then very down. There was nevertheless an air of abandon come over the place. Berlin was of course full of foreigners who had rushed in to reap the benefit—and there were two hundred thousand refugees who had gained admission and by some fantastic means were rich and it was they who ate all the caviar and pheasant, while the hungry Germans outside were peering in at the window.

All Russians eat enormously—and Scandinavians I believe—I imagine it is the intense cold of the winter that demands it. I always remember the quantities of hors d'oeuvres eaten by all those northerners in restaurants in Paris before they began the real meal at all.

Life however in Berlin then was at the height of heights—that is to the highest pitch of sophistication and abandon. None of us had seen anything quite like the spectacle—the psychological themes were incredible—and a record of life from that standpoint alone would make remarkable reading—honesty driven out of countenance or so it seemed. But it was a vast fury of life and had to be gone through with that way—and life being life—is taken as it is. It will never be that way again—not there—and by now the thing has shifted to other cities—New York being one of these conspicuous in these times.

All of us lived however—in whatever degree it became necessary to do—some of them went almost under from dissipation, but all of them by little miracles recovered and went on to some other form of experience. I was the only painter and I worked every day as usual and joined my German friends afternoons and evenings for diversion. I was with Rönnebeck much of course in that period too—for there was never a time when I would not be likely to, since we were firm solid friends from the 1912–13 epoch and still are friends though the form has changed to his life. He is removed at a distance in Denver with a family of his own. How the end of that period changed everything really. It was toward the end of 1922 I was walking about in an exhibition of musical instruments ancient and modern with Eva Gauthier.[74] She handed me some clippings that took my breath and sent my eyes swimming—these clippings announcing the death of the young American singer Alice Miriam whom she did not know. I walked away and, finding myself in front of an ancient spinet, struck a few notes as I had to do something to stem the tide and loosen the tension. "I didn't know you knew her," said Eva very earnestly. "Yes, I knew her," was all I could say then. That was the death of talented and precious little Alice Miriam Pinch.

What a blow it was between the eyes—this otherwise so causal news— to us who loved her so and who were so happy that, after all her fierce struggles, she had reached the Metropolitan and had achieved a stellar role with outspoken success—and as a result was taken by Caruso on his last tour as the other soloist. He was so pleased with her voice and liked her so much and she had found him inordinately generous and kind as everyone else seemed to have done.

And by an ill-timed fate another young and talented singer, Mario Laurenti—a baritone with a fine voice also at the Metropolitan, also died. I had heard them both in "Carmen" with Farrar. Charming fellow Laurenti—very fine voice. Alice was a bright, cheerful, naughty little sort of sprite whom we all still love.

1922–23 was what it came to be then. I had come into extra "blessings" and decided I must have a spell of Italian art—so I sent my pictures home from Berlin late that season—1922. I had done a lot of pictures that period and some of them are now in the Howald collection in Columbus.

So I headed for Vienna—to find it all that I had heard of it save of course the spirit very much down. There was little of what was known as Viennese gaiety—no great waltz pieces being written—sure indication that Vienna was down. Only that week a revue had opened called "Wien Lacht Wiedern," or "Vienna laughs again." It was not a remarkable revue, but there is only one place in the world where the revue is at its finest and that is New York.

I regret to say that I recall not many of the pictures I saw there—for one easily forgets the smaller museums—but the eight days were pleasant and gave me a sense of what the charming city would be like at its best.

I moved on at the end of eight days to Florence via Innsbruck and as it was November, enjoyed passing through snow banks with staring Alps buried in snow in the offing. I had to change over to the train coming down from Munich and found a very comfortable train, so comfortable I thought I had made a mistake for second class was very de luxe.

There was an elderly lady in the compartment also on her way to Florence who later on, after the train had started, told the story of her reason for leaving at that time. It was terrible she said—and dangerous. It was the now famous Hitler uprising of that year, the tenth anniversary of which was celebrated on the ninth of November—ten days ago—this year of 1933—with the same Hitler delivering the speech. A very different cast of features the situation has now with ninety percent of the people believing in him.[75]

The train moved on eventually and delivered us duly in Florence— arriving at six o'clock in the morning, so that I was able to locate myself— and get out to see the far-famed Ponte Vecchio first of all—the so much etched Ponte Vecchio—a very simple affair. I think my first disappointment there was in the Arno—for I had never seen a yellow river—having been born on a slowly sweeping solemn one, the Androscoggin in Maine.

Rivers had always been blue or grey or black for me—and to see a yellow river—well it looked ill at first. But I began to get its quality—and soon found that it went superbly with all the old gold Florentine houses—and blue reflections on it were both different and pleasing. Florence is so full of magnificent ghosts that it takes a time to get used to that aspect alone— for you get slowly to see Leonardo, Raphael, Masaccio, Cellini—and all the stupendous galaxy of geniuses. Turning any corner, to come face to face with great masterpieces in the streets and piazzas is in itself overcoming— and it is not long before the grandeur of it all overcomes you and you wonder how much of it you can bear and how much of it you can understand— then of course you soon find you can both bear and understand all of it—and so you settle down—and once you keep the foreigners out of eye—you are all right.

I have written the episode of the *pensione* in which I lived—the Pensione Balestri—but a repetition will be permissible.

Signora Balestri was a clever woman and her family had had this *pensione* for many years. I forget the name of the little plaza—on the banks of the Arno—not far from the Ponte Vecchio on one side and the Uffizi on the other. Signora Balestri was a suave but astute little business woman. She had been married to a German and lived in Germany—either the war brought her home or her husband was killed or something—but she spoke perfect German, she spoke perfect English, perfect French, and of course Italian. The *pensione* was overflowing but as I was to stay weeks—I was given a room—small—facing at the back looking over Florentine roofs— and the pensionaires were international—Germans, Swedes, Danes, Irish, English—and I the American. It was my first experience in a pension and was not over-sympathetic to me—but it was full of all kinds of people and all of them very different. I soon became aware of an exceptional looking man—British—with a very sensitive face—a face in which much suffering was visible. He was obviously a man of cultivation and obviously had served in the war. He always sat at table with his father, mother and sister— all of them distinguished and cultivated looking.

To come quickly to the idea. Letters on the table in the hall disclosed a name I was familiar with and I had with me a book with the same name attached to it, and the book was "Coté de Guermante," and the translator, Capt. K. Scott-Moncrieff, was the gentleman in question.[76] I spoke to him eventually—though I know geniuses and many plain people do not like to be spoken to—but the situation was a permissible one as I was reading his book and caring quite as much for his part of it as I was of the author from whom it was translated—so much so that I called it "his book" when I spoke of it to him. He said he carried a volume with him everywhere and translated it piece by piece in street cars, libraries, wherever he happened to be.

Sadly this gentleman with a fine face and breeding back of his whole manner died without finishing the last volume of Proust—which was taken up by someone else.

I was impressed of course and a bit awed by the Italian soldiers and there was some sort of an army station or barracks across the plaza from the *pensione.* I was made still more aware of it all by Leo Stein who was living out at Settignano, who warned me never to speak the word *"Fascismo."* Say "bundle" if you speak of it—or the English fasces—never say *Fascismo* for they don't know what you are saying of it and they are very volatile and disagreeable—and of course it was in its great beginning—*Fascismo*—just that year.

But I knew nothing of *Fascismo* then—and little about it now—save that being in Germany or Bavaria at the moment and seeming somehow to look like a native—is it my fine green plush hat—I bought in Paris in 1913—and never found a real place to wear it until this year? Or is it my mountain cape, or is it both? But I get the N.S.D.A.P. salute very often and never know quite what to do—because in quite the same way I never can cross myself in a Catholic church and I frequently go in them—especially in Europe.[77] Go into the Cathedral of Chartres for a half hour and watch the blue windows get bluer as the day flushes and fades and it will seem as if you have to cross yourself.

Well all that is aside—I was getting into Florence thick and fast—and the faster, the thicker it became, for Florence is a place where you have to look at pictures—if pictures are what you may be caring about—and four or five hours a day of looking at pictures will cloud both your mind and your eye thickly. I have also recalled the remark of a singular looking English woman in a restaurant elsewhere, I having offered her a light for her cigarette—the husband or companion—and I should say by the manners, husband, having lighted his cigarette then blown the match out. And the woman said to me, "I hear there are a lot of pictures here in Florence. Are they really worth seeing?" "That would depend, madam, entirely," I replied, "on how much one likes pictures." Pictures it is in Florence or nothing—pictures and sculpture—and now after ten years I should like to do them all over again. And it is only twenty-four hours or so from here—for in ten years even the eye changes its mind about a lot of things, and the clearer it gets the more it sees and senses differently—and I really can look at pictures now without being overcome by them and learning the pictures in a place like Florence—or like the Louvre—is a work all by itself and still more so if you know the process of the making as any painter is bound to do.

Florence is therefore the university for the eye and you must come there having done all the preliminary visualizing—and you must have patience and endurance—patience to pierce through the always difficult lighting of churches and galleries, and endurance to stand the dreadful cold that permeates all Italian churches and galleries—for there is no heating system in the galleries and the guards stand about with their overcoats on—warming hands at charcoal braziers. You will get church ague and museum neuritis very readily—so this next sentence should be written as a prescription. Time your visits to museums in summer—if you can—because summer heat may warm museums and churches and nothing will this side of an inferno in winter.

The worst of all is the light question—and the light always having been the same, how in heaven's name did the masters ever see to do them? Yet there they are, and they probably had brown eyes.

And there is the question of the "droll type" from England and the drollest of them all get to Italy and the Riviera. "Are they really worth seeing—the pictures?" They are.

Another question comes—what do people get out of pictures who know nothing of picture making and the problems of making them? At least the student of art can fill himself to the hair with the interest in the problem. The person who may have painted a little gets of course more—and novels written by esthetes are these days as full of references to painting, chiefly Dutch painting at present. It used to be Italian. Now it is Vermeer. And so you must sleep well and eat well if you are to look at pictures for it is another equivalent of a prize fight for the eye and mind.

Florence is the Olympic game center of the arts—and there is nothing that was ever done they couldn't and didn't do. After you have done the rounds of all the churches and the museums once you will know just how much you can stand, and then you begin over again—and eight weeks of Florence will make you glad you did it and will make you wonder if you can ever do it again for it is like an American Thanksgiving dinner for the eye—maybe once a year you can do it till you get a stomach full. The worst for me was the voluptuous sense of design and ornamentation. I am not one of those who thinks cloth of gold and velvet the last word in perfect experience, because I care more for metals and stones—for ice and cold winds of the north—for gothic rigidity—and gothic loftiness—the difference between the south nature and the north nature I guess.

And my mind turned after all this jeweled grandeur to the severe simplicities and depth of Masaccio. What a boy that was—after all a boy—only twenty-seven when he died, the only one that has even done what seemed to me a natural and plausible Christ, the only one that seemed imbued with pure piety and pure mysticism. Go to the Church of the Carmine and see the fresco of the "Tribute Money" and there is all that I am meaning. The true Christ on earth in the midst of men.

You go to the museum of Fra Angelico and you have all that the glory of heaven can mean in painting. The rest is cultivation without much else behind it—witness the Raphael madonnas—empty as a windbag.

I used to go up to Fiesole every now and then to get a breath of air, look down on Florence, come back, and begin again. I was sitting on the long flight of steps at my first visit to Fiesole—for it is a bit of a tug up the hill after you get to the town itself, to the monastery of St. Francis. I was seating myself under the cypresses—and just below the tableted poem of Carducci, seeing how much I could read of it—watching the mists come and

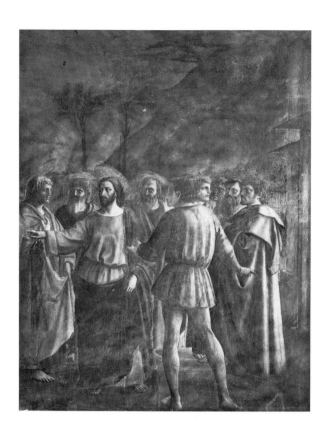

Masaccio, Christ surrounded by the apostles, detail
from *The Tribute Money*, Brancacci Chapel, S. Maria
del Carmine, Florence, Italy (photo: Alinari/Art
Resource, New York).

go down over Florence and the Arno.[78] It was late in the afternoon and the sky was reddening somewhat, putting the whole valley in a kind of copperous oxidized glow—little to be seen from there save Giotto's tower—when I heard strains of music coming down the stairs from the chapel above—and I knew it was vesper time. The music drew me to the chapel and I went in. The monks were just beginning special vespers for one of the saints—one of the women saints, just which I have forgotten—and a young and very affable monk with curly black hair and something of a faun's face stood at the door more or less welcoming visitors. He was suave and gracious. I entered the chapel and heard superb voices old and young in behind the screen—full throated sopranos and deep sonorous baritones. The music was ancient—Palestrina perhaps—all old music is restful because it is so balanced, so made for the "repose of the soul." That was the end of that visit.

I went again several times to get the utmost of the pictures—and the next time the faunish monk addressed me—in pieces of several languages because he knew I could not speak Italian. The effect of his remarks was this: "It is beautiful up here is it not? Away from the world, we live a beautiful life here within these walls." And his next remark flustered me a little—this in the form of flattery since it was being addressed to me: "Wouldn't you like to be one of us—we are fifty-one here—and you would be fifty-two." I hardly knew what to answer and fancied of course all the splendour of his meaning—could see myself within the walls—and thought—yes it would be nice being away from all the struggles of things. I thanked the faun for his invitation and said I must think of it—I told no one of this—and thought it must be one of those treasured secrets that come to one now and then.

After a third or fourth visit—the same vivacious monk was always at the door—I observed that he was not above taking little contributions from the strangers so I too added a little bit for the idea of St. Francis.

Eventually I did tell the little story at the *pensione* one evening—in German, because I was with two German boys and two Danish girls who spoke German also—and after I had finished the handsomer of the two Germans laughed and quite in my face—raised a finger of a hand that had never worked—and said facetiously in German, "O no—that doesn't go—I am to be the fifty-second—you will have to be the fifty-third"—and the joke came out—the faun was proselytizing a bit. The faun had also said, "You can live here with us—and have a beautiful life to the end of your days—or you can be sent out into the world to any part you might wish to go."

He is probably still there, the faun—probably not as vivacious, he is ten years older—and neither the German nor myself can be fifty-one or fifty-two in the order—because doubtless someone else has taken those places.

The order used to walk twice a week around the hills of Fiesole—and you saw the fifty of them—led by older monks with long grey beards, followed by the younger in the thirties, those of the twenties coming at the last.

There was a German art critic living in Settignano in the home of the resident priest. He was an acquaintance of Leo Stein, who lived much further down beyond the villa where Duse and D'Annunzio were said to have lived[79]—and from the outside all you saw were those always death sensing tall cypresses, made so thoroughly impossible to the eye by Böcklin's dreadful painting, "The Isle of Death," of which he had made replicas—and if I am not mistaken for the retired Kaiser. As for my feeling, did Böcklin ever paint anything but terrible pictures? "Kitsch"—a very expressive German word—to the last.

The esthete and his wife, who were living in the home of the priest, invited me to spend Saturday and Sunday with them—they living in the end rooms of the priestly residence, behind walls of course with plenty of garden. Sunday morning I listened to the mass in a secret closet, entered from the house with a little window looking in at the church, presumably for servants. The priest was an observing, clever man—very amiable, very courteous—no longer young. The spiritual guide of the village—and as also often happens being leader—something of a despot—and ruled the town. There was nothing remarkable about the esthete—or art critic—he was one of many such—who was writing books on Cézanne and cubism.

And this brings me to a visit to Charles Loeser, a man from Brooklyn who had lived most of his life in Florence—and had, besides a fine Bronzino which is the only other picture I remember, a music room—for his wife was an excellent musician and supported a well-known trio or quartet.[80] In this music room there were a lot of Cézannes—I don't remember how many—but I do remember their lustrousness and a kind of relief I got from all the ponderous elegance and grandeur of the Renaissance pictures.

I was twenty minutes late for this visit as I was a stranger in Florence and had never been in that part of town. Mr. Loeser's reception disturbed me a little—because his first remark was, "Good morning—you are late. I said eleven thirty didn't I? Well—a—anyhow come in. I have another appointment here at twelve—but come in you can look at the pictures meanwhile," and I was left with the pictures.

The twelve o'clock appointment of Mr. Loeser being finished he returned to me in a much more affable mood—and invited me to stay to lunch. There will be something or other he said and there was—plenty of spaghetti I remember. I was wanting to see the other remarkable collection of Cézannes in Florence—was the name Fabbri?—but as those things take a lot of machination I never got to see them.[81] I met no one in Florence because that too is a lot of work—I was through Leo Stein to have met the writer of "South Wind" who was then living there—and was given his address—made a call and found him out.[82] Outside of the pictures there is nothing for the stranger to do save know the foreigners and do teas—and maybe dinners if you are important enough, but I never was—for dinners—not dinners of "special" people.

I did go to Berenson's, however, with Leo one Sunday afternoon—walked with Leo from his house—a nice walk, and was ushered into an elegant villa through a large garden. We were early but the butler said the family would soon be there and we were ushered into a huge library with miles of books—and Italian pictures everywhere else in the house.

The process of tea was begun. Mrs. Berenson—a most agreeable woman—came in and presently Mr. Berenson—a very sensitive frail man—and he and Leo proceeded at once to a violent conversation.[83] I had seated myself near Mrs. Berenson and the tea things and enjoyed being near and with her.

It was not long before there was a perfect volley of words between Mr. B. and Leo—and then I heard Mr. B. say, "No Leo, what you mean is not experimental but experiential" or vice versa—and a battle had begun. Leo meant nothing of the kind—and so on and on it went and I wonder if either of them took any tea. Mrs. B. said to me, "O it's always like that with them—they are fond of each other but they should never get together."

I seem to see the end of Florence and the pictures there as it was getting on toward Christmas and I had planned Christmas in Rome—and knew I would find Maurice Sterne there at least.[84] I moved on to Assisi because outside of Masaccio—Piero della Francesca was my main idol.

Some notes can be inserted here.[85]

Arezzo

Leaving Florence on the two o'clock train I had little hope of arriving much before sundown to achieve the object of my visit—namely of course the Chiesa di San Francesco. At four o'clock, however, after a series of handsome vistas of dry, parched, and very classical looking landscapes between Florence and Arezzo, the main pleasure I remember was an amazing blue house—an intense sky blue it was against all the brown and silver scene.

Getting myself installed in the Stella d'Italia, in a large-sized *piccola camera*, I went straight to the church of San Francesco to get what I could of that day—and down behind the altar—there to receive the first powerful shaft of these elegant, austere, distinguished, and, in a final word, magnificent frescoes.

After all the affluent rhetoric of Botticelli and the deeper Ghirlandaio—it was like looking at rich ripe fruits after a perfect surfeit of extravagant and exotic flora. Less metaphysical than Masaccio and the frescoes in the Novella—I had expected of course severity and reserve—coolness and pure intellectuality.[86] Not cynical like Mantegna—or the almost perverse Pollaiuolo, dignified spiritually even as the lofty Angelico—remaining on earth however, this clear brightness away from the machinations of men—a kind of Buddhistic nobility—discreet dismissal of

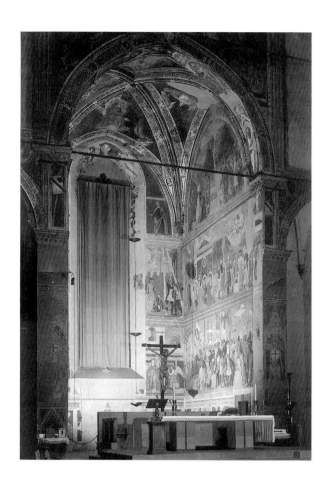

Piero della Francesca, frescoes on the left of the
apse, S. Francesco, Arezzo, Italy (photo: Scala/Art
Resource, New York).

extraneous ornamentation—and hyper decorative purposes—and of superfluous detail.

It seemed as if here was perfection of meaning, of accomplishment—premier in thought—certainly too original to be accepted even in their times without severe qualifications.

Incomparable sense of arrangement, majesty of style, most superior comprehension of simplicity—everything cut down to its last line and form, masterful sense of pageantry in the themes—and of wall spacing—all going to a center of group sensations joined in a single movement—none of the intrusion of illustration indulged in to such excess as by Gozzoli in the Palazzo Riccardi or even Lippi in the Novella.[87] That could not have happened with Piero or a man like Masaccio because they were vastly deeper men, for they knew the meaning of reticence, and of omission.

What handsome men and women, horses, superior touches of landscape set off by matchless groupings of hill town architecture. Coolness—hardness even, light, movement without contortion, and none of those florid exuberances so wearing to the eye—here, the emotions too lofty for inferior consideration. These decorations march straight to the acme of satisfaction and praise—something to be remembered when the rest may be forgotten—like a mass in a sense after so much opera.

Next Morning

Best light of all it seemed to me for Piero—clear, cold, hard, testing these frescoes in every way from the warm last glow of yesterday, when they seemed thinner—after the two visits of today.

A curious disregard of excessive detail—I first thought—and yet I remarked at close range that even single hairs were painted on the legs of the horses along the line of the silhouette—and the introduction of some swans in the river that passes in and out of the brown and white landscape—all so tarnished looking, like old pure metals—between the bodies of the two horses. How they shine out in all their calm grandeur, these frescoes—such perfection and unification in the right section of the "Morte e Sepoltura di Adamo," the finishing lunette of the grand right wall—so full of austere peace and simplicity, above the "Disfatta di Mas-

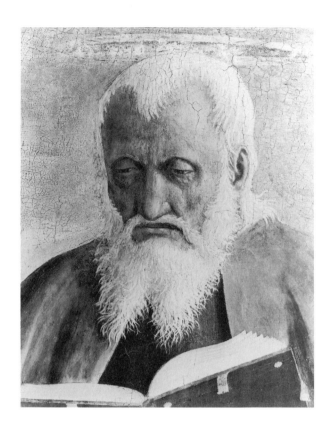

Piero della Francesca, head of an apostle, detail
from a panel of the *Sant' Agostino Altarpiece*, The Frick
Collection, New York, photo, Marsden Hartley
Collection, Yale Collection of American Literature,
Beinecke Rare Book and Manuscript Library, Yale
University. This was acquired by Hartley, who may
have recognized a resemblance between his own face
and that of the apostle.

senzio," and the beautiful appreciation of the silence of a city to the left, in the "Invenzione e Verificazione della Santa Croce."[88]

How they shine out in all their calm grandeur in the world of ideas these masterpieces of Piero—dominating in a sense like precious stones— the rusty iron hills with the first visitations of winter on the Apennines, in a little city of oxidized bronze. Arezzo is therefore a great name in my memory and Piero one of the few very great experiences—as to whether one feels great religious emotions in Piero, it is of no consequence. He was a first grade intellectual in art—and his pictures have all that great pictures are meant to have, and he settles so many of the esthetic problems of that time by his strange coolness and aloofness. These pictures live in a world of deep conviction and you are aware that something profound has happened, and this is not always so.

Probably a no more startling sense of the immediateness of an idea can be found than in his "Resurrezione" in the Borgo San Sepolcro—which I did not get to see because I was made aware of the difficulties of that time. A great many pictures can be given up—but not these of Piero—or the ever impelling work of Masaccio in the Carmine and his crucifixion in the Novella.

Mountains these men were of intelligence, taste, feeling, and good judgment—both satisfied that the little well done was worth a vastitude of indifferent or merely skillful picture making. Perfect union of intellect and the inner vision which, for want of a better name, is called "soul."

Cafe Constanti, Arezzo

I have described in other papers—the episode of the huge Italian with white hair—appearing German to me—and saying if you are going to Rome—don't fail to get off at Orvieto, for the wine there is famous—and never so good as in Orvieto itself.[89] I have also told of the meeting of a Japanese gentleman—at the station in Arezzo while we were both waiting for the train to Rome—he to go on and I to get off at Arezzo—and of his saying how singular the women of Arezzo's frescoes were to the Japanese eye so unfeminine, as they are indeed quite masculine in appearance.[90]

It was then Christmas week—and the fatigue of pictures was over me. Is there anything more fatiguing—when they are good? Nothing.

It was pleasant to come into a city again—and to walk up and down the Corso, between the Porto del Popolo and the huge ugly monument to Victor Emmanuel.

There was a plentifulness of good looking Italian men—mostly offi-cers—and a dearth of women. Latin women do not walk the streets for any reason—and the better they are the less are they to be seen—only once did I really see them and that was in a smart tea room, the name of which I have forgotten—but they were out that afternoon at least with their hus-bands—mostly officers—and it is a rich picture of life this sort of Italian makes—for they are full and voluptuous—large eyed and very handsome.

I found Maurice Sterne duly in his atelier—and there was a model on the stand. He was working hard on life-size figures then. "Where did you get that marvelous creature?" I said. "O she is one of the family that come from Anticoli, Corrado. There is a whole family of them—sons and daughters, and they all pose. Better come to Anticoli," Maurice said—but time was short—only a week and Anticoli had already found itself on the aesthetic map—and I never cared for colonies.

There was talk of the midnight mass—for Christmas in a well-known church then and everyone was going—that is, everyone of the group. I was all set for something unusual as Maurice had said the music was famous there. Well it was bad that year—and I was not interested in hearing Mas-senet's "Meditation from 'Thaïs'" in any church or anywhere else. Massenet in Paris is fine and should be heard in Paris.

That week I seemed to see nothing but the Coliseum—and decided after my first visit that Rome or any other place could offer no more—so I sat on the stones of the Coliseum most of the week.

Of course the Sistine Chapel gave you a headache because it is the wrong place to be looking for pictures—on a ceiling—but I did see them and felt they were almost as good seeing them at the Alinari Library in Florence as they were on the ceiling—for they are in the end colourless—

and they are in the end sculpture. The Last Judgment on one of the walls—well, very grand—very tormented and very hard to see. When you have walked down the long corridors of the Vatican Gallery—you are fagged when you get to the Sistine Chapel, and I had had a rich draft of Michelangelo in the Medici Chapel in Florence anyhow, and the many unfinished statues in the museum which Rodin had looked hard at—attempting to make an art of bodies emerging out of vague masses—which was all right in Michelangelo's case, as they were never finished.

The holidays finished with a vision of the Sicilian players in Rome who were then in vogue, in rustic comedy of a most homely and invigorating sort.

I was to take ship in the Fabre Line *La Patria* at Monaco—and the end of the Italian visit in Naples.

Naples—what a contrast to Florence the patrician, Rome the patrician—all this Neapolitan roughness, noise, filth, picturesquely common they all were. I saw nothing much there in Naples in the two days—I foolishly let Pompeii and the museum side of Naples slip—but I couldn't seem to do any more of that—and it was all people and dogs, people and cats, people and people—much singing and carousing and an air of everlasting childish gaiety—and everybody looked sort of dangerous also—which had its charm as everywhere.

It is enjoyable being in the presence of murderers and thieves when they are not murdering or thieving, for when they are not doing either of these things they are playing as they are in all big cities—and I know their types in Italy, France, and Germany—and Marseilles—and Marseilles is a country by itself. O the wild rough gaiety of the Marseillaises when they are not murdering and thieving—the "ladies" in the rue de la Loge who will snatch your hat as you walk by—and when you learn that a franc will get it back—you save yourself a lot of blasphemy in several languages. Or if you are a "fresh alec" foreigner you can have much more than you had bargained for. You can be cracked over the head nicely or be stripped to the hide—if you lose your head, and the "fresh alec" usually does—it is usually what he likes to do—well the "ladies" know how to begin all things and their pals will finish it for you neat and nice, and no two policemen—

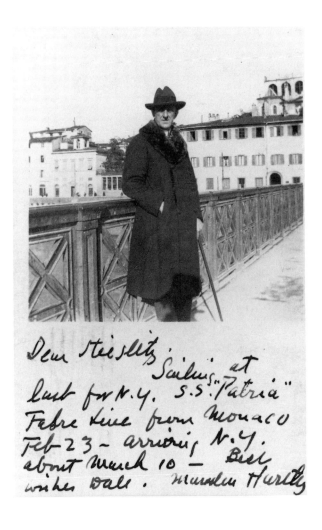

Dear Stieglitz; Sailing at
last for N.Y. S.S. "Patria"
Fabre Line from Monaco
Feb 23 – arriving N.Y.
about March 10 – Best
wishes Dall. Marsden Hartley

Hartley's postcard to Alfred Stieglitz from Florence,
dated February 15, 1924, Marsden Hartley
Collection, Yale Collection of American Literature,
Beinecke Rare Book and Manuscript Library,
Yale University.

and they always walk in twos in the rough quarter of Marseilles—can do anything about you or them. And even though the policemen there are chiefly Corsicans—therefore afraid of nothing—and the Marseillaises are afraid of nothing like them, every now and then a policeman gets his too—having witnessed a grand funeral procession of a lately done-in policeman there—knifed or shot to death—I forget which. Murderers and thieves at play—just children.

We had embarked at the little harbour of Monaco—a most pleasing way of taking ship—for you are taken in a tender from the quiet little *quai*—and out with the ship that is waiting for you. But before you leave—and in guide book tone—you must be sure you have seen the marine museum in Monaco, one of the best in the world. It is the only place I have seen scientific drawings that had the quality of art in them—an old longing of mine—for I am always wondering why the scientist is never enough of an artist to do these things right—in the manner of Audubon for example. But here the drawings were excellent—and had the peculiar quality of mysticity—which all sea forms have—plus a fine esthetic sense of them. They were gouache drawings of polyps chiefly—and gouache is by all means the best medium for this kind of drawing.

I should have seen the marine museum also in Naples but that too slipped me—but there is always the feeling when you are beating about that you can be doing it again one day and pick up what you missed or what you may have forgotten.

The small list of passengers in second class, perhaps forty people, looked promising as passengers seldom do—for there were a number of typical American boys and girls going home—and we all settled down to what we thought was going to be a nice journey by the "wonderful southern route"—lovely weather they said all the way.

The time came in Naples for shoving off—and to our horror there began to come flocks and flocks of the most unappetizing looking people—women with handkerchiefs on their heads, carrying heaps of bedding on their backs bound for the Italies of the United States—and all of them into the second class—all smelling of garlic and wet babies and themselves. So beautiful they were however—that their beauty seemed to take the curse off all the rest of their appearances.

"This will not be so lovely a trip," I guessed to one or other of the Americans standing near—and it was not.

But there was Palermo, first of all—after having a good look at Vesuvius, no small pleasure for anyone who likes mountains, and volcanoes—dead or alive. A lady in Cannes had said, "You must be sure to see the mosaics at Monreale"—and so Palermo held something special.

The ship settled down in the harbour of Palermo and there was a flutter of all but naked boys diving for small coins—any coin, any boy—and you were paid for the coin you threw by seeing one dive—wait until it got fairly down—and when the flash of light followed it—then springing over the side like porpoises—coming up with it in their teeth and a *grazie* to close the bargain.

The hills were all lovely brown at Palermo and the swaying green of the waters and the palms toned it off to the pleasantness.

There was a priest on board who had something special on his mind—and a church was mentioned—and some of the Americans followed. I was to miss this and found myself in another little crew and a church was again spoken of—and with mosaics on my mind I thought I was being taken to them. I should have joined the priest—for he went straight to the masterpieces of Monreale which is out of the town. I got stuck in a little church that had only tiny bits—and I missed out on some of the masterpieces of the world—by not knowing or caring rightly at the time—and only the reading of a historical sketch later on revealed to me what I had missed—and Palermo is a place I am not likely to get to again—and of course there was Taormina and Stra not to enjoy—Taormina of great beauty and bad sewage I had afterward learned—so if you miss one thing, you miss another.

O the charm of the southern route—how terrible in all ways—three hundred or more being sea-sick every minute all over everything—and you if you were not careful. After bad weather almost as bad as any northern voyage, shortage of coal, shortage of water, sewer gas coming up from the wash-stands, and the air of mutiny among the stewards—a landing in the Providence River to wait twenty-four hours there. For what, no one could learn—politics and manipulation, certainly—some evasion of law that could be managed in Rhode Island and not in New York apparently—which cost the Fabre line a thousand dollars in railroad fares as they had booked their passengers to New York—but we also learned that as we were paying ninety dollars for our passages, these Italians were paying a hundred and seventy for theirs, so the line was still making money.

That was the end of that period.

I was enabled to return again in 1925—and I don't remember much about this—save that I painted some dark landscapes in monochrome tone in the studio of George Biddle.[91]

I had come across Louise Bryant at that time—long after Jack Reed's death and Louise's life in Russia. Jo Davidson, whom I came across in the street, said, "Someone is looking for you and wants so much to see you. Louise Bryant—she has married again—and this is her address and her phone." I called Louise and there was a joyous meeting—please come out to tea this afternoon she had said I want you to meet Bill—and then you must come out next week and stay a week. And William Bullitt and I liked each other from the start and there were fine times.[92] They had I think recently returned from Turkey of which Bullitt was very fond, and even though Louise liked it too she was not well there. The decline and fall of Turkey had taken place and there were many Turkish palaces going to ruin—Bullitt thought then of buying one and so they looked at many—and at once were met by a fascinating little Turkish boy of good but reduced family and were so smitten with his perfect oriental manners and the reception he gave them. It all ended by buying no palaces but by bringing the boy to Paris to educate him. Refik boy was a most engaging infant of perhaps nine—and though no one but Bullitt could talk with him in Turkish—he was irresistible to everyone by his elegant deportment.[93]

They were living in the Elinor Glyn house—and I was to sleep eventually—or try to sleep—in the great canopied divan of the duchess of Hollywood later to be.[94] Folds and folds of plum and pistachio taffeta looped and draped about the bed—was something new for me—and much fun

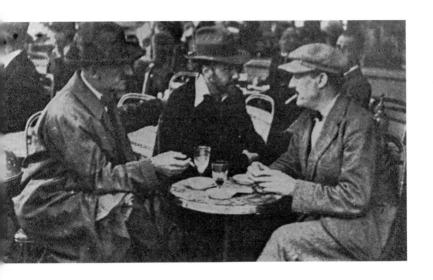

"Prominent Montparnassians," photograph from
unknown English-language newspaper, ca. 1924,
Marsden Hartley Memorial Collection, Museum of
Art, Bates College. Left to right: Hartley, Ezra
Pound, and Fernand Léger, Café du Dôme, Paris.

was had by all on the subject, I never having slept under canopies of taffeta, with a small Chinese lamp on the wall, and a bed so soft it felt indecent under me—for beating about the world beds get softer by their degrees of hardness. No small hotel in Paris will offer you swansdown no matter where you go—a camp cot with nothing on is an Elysium in comparison—but you learn to sleep anywhere—beating about.

Bill and Louise had been to Egypt and that winter that we were all playing about the fireplace with a sapphire as large as a robin's egg and as blue as all the thousand and one nights. I had played with little gems in course of time but never with a king's diadem piece—one of the best it was and must have come from Cashmere—is it not Cashmere from which the best sapphires come? Eventually it was set in platinum with small diamonds on the under side—and so we didn't play with it anymore for Louise could then wear it, and I wondered so often if it would ever be stolen but it was so huge it looked like a piece of stained glass—and no one but an expert jewel thief would know its value.

Biddle had come to my room for I was in bed then with "charcuterie" poisoning—the result of overindulgence in amazing hors d'oeuvres—served in a well-known Paris restaurant. George said, "I am leaving for three weeks for the Tours region—and I would be pleased if you would accept my studio for that time"—and I wanted to get to work. George returned and kindly said, "If you think you could work in the room with anyone—I would be glad to have you stay on," and I stayed on—George being a nice person. George would work a while then stop and play the flute—and he played it nicely—nice old French airs and such—and then he would go to work again on his sort of Gauguinesque pastorals fused with pointillism. I was working on some New Mexico landscapes and some fish pieces that were eventually to be called "Chez Prunier," for I used to study the fish in Prunier's window after I had been to the window of Van Cleef and Arpels in the Place Vendôme to look at the sapphires and diamonds, which I often did. I always got something out of looking at clear stones, and still do—though from all the other stones—which I looked at less—I looked at star sapphires more—as having more intellect and more

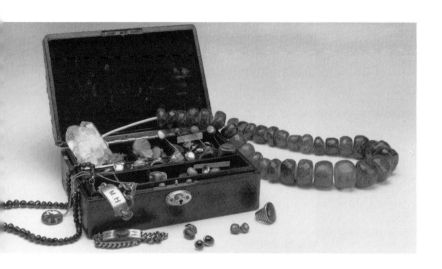

Hartley's jewelry box, Marsden Hartley Memorial
Collection, Museum of Art, Bates College, photo by
Melville McLean. Hartley was an occasional
collector of gems, beads, and crystals. He also
collected "identity" bracelets, at least three of which
were found among his effects when he died.

distinction—the greatest stones in the whole range I think—devoid of oriental sensuality—even though they come from the Orient.

Things got better then—for through Bullitt a "syndicate" was arranged with understanding friends of his in New York whereby I was to be released for four years and go on without the usual disturbance—I to deliver, according to my own suggestion, a certain number of pictures in the year—so that I could feel I was earning my living thereby avoiding gifts.[95] I went south, remembering a lovely visit to Keith and Hutchins Hapgood whom I have known since Provincetown's "big summer." I remembered Vence from that visit, went there, and took a house quite to my needs and choice with an adorable French landlord—a cripple who could not walk—but lived in a wheelchair and had a little motor made that would get him up the hill and into town so he could have something of a life to offset his plight—and in spite of his own and that of his wife, who was declining from T. B., kept up the most inspiring freshness of spirit.

Monsieur Debroux-Perus [?] was a most charming person—and I am sorry I didn't make more of him now—for he remains in my memory as the nicest most engaging personality of all that were there. There was a group of American painters to play with—four, to be exact, who had all been by chance at Provincetown and had lived there for years—there being Miss Mars and Miss Squire—the subjects of the portrait "Miss Furr and Miss Skeene" by Gertrude Stein—as well as Oliver Chaffee and Ada Gilmore.[96] They were also a part of the famous "big summer" at the end of Massachusetts—what an end!—and a number of haughty English—a woman with many dogs, a woman with two dogs, and a woman with not more than one dog, but she wore a baroque pearl in one ear and a turquoise in the other—and had a talent for flowers. Everybody grew flowers and two other English girls had a carnation farm. The country around Vence itself was nice to look at but not to paint—but Gattière and Cannes further over were quite wonderful. I went to Gattière for two weeks at that time trying to paint Italian alpine profiles—but no one liked them—I am sure. They sit in storage waiting to be either washed out or gone over—so I guess—it's washed out.

I didn't get much out of any of the Riviera save Cannes which remains in my memory as the nicest place I was ever in—it was quiet there in summer—as they hadn't then begun to build the summer casino to attract summer tourists. They hadn't begun to popularize Jaun-le-Pins, and Antibes was still the rendezvous of quiet artists.

The rest of the Riviera was all "Girofli-Girofla" to me—and of course Nice was the most G. G. of them all. To enjoy Nice you must have been there when the grand old girls and boys of seventy and eighty were still coming—with their jet capes, and marabou ruffs, many ruffles, little lapdogs, and the men with diamond horseshoe cravat pins, waxed mustaches, black and white checked trousers, white spats, and white grey top-hats and bowlers. You must have had all these to get Nice at its most amusing. Now it is all faded gigolos and dancers.

None of all that at Cannes—one of the few places of any kind in the world surely—certainly one of the only resorts in the world where the atmosphere was completely free.

The beautiful sharp blue profiles of the Esterel and the wide expanse of quiet sea gave you the feeling that it was the one place in the world which was "open"—almost all places have a closed feeling of some sort. Two wondrous beaches—the upper one surely two miles long, the other one below the hotels beginning at the Casino—surely a mile or nearly so—and the sun bathing perfect in both of them. "Vieux" Cannes upon the hill keeping its old local flavour and all the rest—villas and hotels of the most expensive kind—costly yachts moored at the *quais*—and you saw "upper" gentlemen coming down to them in cars from the tennis courts elegantly disappearing into their sea-palaces. Next to all this—the little place with its local fishing life—old sailors mending nets, their sturdy wiry wives often with them also mending—such a pretty little unit it is of this sort of life—and, though it is within a stone's throw of the most expensive way of life anywhere in the Riviera, at least you walk about among the little softly coloured boats—steel grey—plum black—offset with just the right blue or the right ochre and red. There is "Marguerite," or "Yvonne," or "Lolette"—and all their girl friends resting on their keels—waiting to be

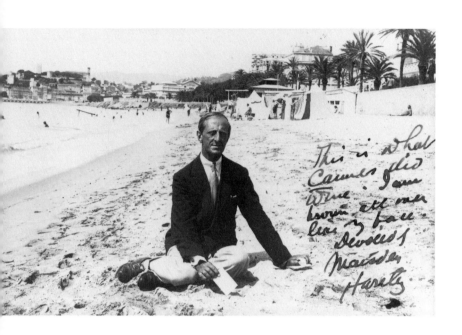

Hartley on beach at Cannes, postcard, ca. 1925,
Marsden Hartley Collection, Yale Collection of
American Literature, Beinecke Rare Book and
Manuscript Library, Yale University.

called to sea again for fishing—and that's a form of life that can be enjoyed from Palermo to Bremerhaven if you know it.

You can enjoy the life of Cannes just as much, and probably more than the richest person there, if your means are ever so small—and there is the advantage in this case of falling into the life of the place itself—and the people of Cannes are very sympathetic. Cannes is the only place I know of on the whole Riviera that offers perfect rest—for the eye, the mind, and the body. If you want the cheapest picture of life known to mankind go to Monte Carlo. Sit about under the trees and observe the saddest of all types of human beings—men and women—the saddest the women—who are past forty and on to seventy—eyes staring into space, cheeks hollowed with anxiety—the women clinging to their diamonds, being all they have left, crawling out every morning waiting for the casino to open to get at the table once again.

You get this at Nice too—but somehow Nice is a place that has a life of its own away from the gaming tables and Monte Carlo has not. What a vision of defeat these women are—I noted women chiefly because defeated men are sort of natural and you find them everywhere—but no woman wants to be or should be defeated and most of these strange dark women are.

None of this at Cannes—for the theatre of life there has the note of light opera—and it always seems as if someone were about to sing—and the light is always exceptional there also.

You can see snow on the palms on the Riviera too if you like—and you are not supposed to—just as you can see snow on the orange and lemon trees in California. Snow on orange blossoms is not really to be missed—but no Californian will let you believe this. What is it makes the Californian so egotistic—I wonder—it was to me a loss—that is, south of San Francisco—save the wondrous beach of Coronado. You can freeze in all these places—again something they will not have you believe—all perfect places have their disappointments. If you take them as they are you are not disappointed but you are always told how perfect they are. The reading of tourist prospectuses is one of the joys of the world—it is like operetta in prose—all so flowery and heavenlike.

The time was up for Vence—a series of still lifes that were, some of them, at their best and some landscape variations that did not come off as they were to be wished—for subjects must be lived into—and two weeks at the Gorges du Loup and two weeks at Gattière were not enough. I don't remember if I went up to look at Aix before moving—but I think I just moved, dog and all. Someone had told me of a small hotel run by an Italian married to a Scotch woman—with three very handsome Italian Scotch children—what a mixture.

Aix-en-Provence, outside of its modern traditions, is a fine old town— a bit of Roman ruin here and there—otherwise rich in seventeenth century elegance, superb houses of the period, and many famous doors—which are the special joy of architectural students. It lives a very solid life of its own—and is hardly aware of its great modern tradition—there is a small monument to Zola—and there is a plaque of Cézanne by Renoir at a fountain. The Cézanne studio takes up all the rest of the outer world's attention.

Aix-en-Provence of course kicks itself for its official stupidity of the time—and not having the something like sixty or seventy canvases offered to it by Cézanne himself. But who could there have been at that time who would be able to understand the difficult Cézanne and his remarkable inventions? No one. Cézanne was a lower bourgeois native—his father was first a hat maker and later turned banker—and, amazing as it is for the kind of family, let the son alone after the usual attempts at finding a profession for the strange son. Cézanne was wealthy therefore—and was left free of monetary distress, otherwise he would surely have starved as the poverty ridden van Gogh was almost later to do further up in Provence at Arles, St. Rémy, and all that.

There is nothing therefore in Aix to remind its own world that a great painter was among them. He had been to Paris, studied somewhat in the schools, found no sympathy, and returned to Aix to make a new art— a museum equivalent to impressionism as he called it—he now in the Louvre—the last place he ever hoped to enter as a celebrity.

You will find a commodious studio there—occupied now chiefly by foreigners who have students' flair for the tradition—a most commodious affair it is—where a few relics still remain of the equipment of Cézanne. There are bits of old felt richly coloured which were to form those Venetianlike backgrounds for his still lifes—there is the old coat and beret of Cézanne which he wore at all times, his sketching umbrella, the cast of the cupid that figures in at least one of his still lifes, and that is about all that remains. According to report the palettes of Cézanne and some letters written by Cézanne to his son are in a safe—the letters not being printable until after the son's death—from all accounts little love for the father on the part of the son. The son has been little heard of.

Vollard was probably the first one to step in[97]—and, in the acute nick of time, bought all the pictures there were of Cézanne and they were numbers and numbers for until then no one had wanted them or could see anything at all in them but the ravings of the mad—Cézanne living the life of a recluse and from all accounts being very disagreeable and unsympathetic to the people of his time. He was savage and unsociable—art will often make a painter that way, witness Courbet: the radical exiled for a time for his too radical ideas—to Switzerland—having torn down the monument in the Place Vendôme I believe.

And you regret as you go about in the charming museum at Aix that instead of dozens of still born studies and paintings by the handsome Granet[98]—a native of Aix who had gone to Rome—that you are not to find anything whatever of Cézanne outside of a most ineffectual "academy" by Cézanne—done in the School of Paris—nothing whatever in it to recommend it—no trace of the magic that was later to come out of the painful isolation.

Cézanne was of Italian extraction—Cezani was the original name— something of the great tradition being brought in by atavism—and a strange new, wonderfully revealing work begun—ideas that were to make the world of painting over again and give modernism its next powerful start. There is no modern picture that has not somehow or other been built upon these new principles. The story is all clear now—the bridge from impressionism to all later modernism having been built until the invention of surrealism and calligraphy. To make a monument of an apple—that was Cézanne's accomplishment—and to show the way to colour perception invented by him. "When the colour harmonizes the design becomes precise"—"all art is based on the cone, the sphere, and the cylinder," etc.

The country about Aix is very rich and original looking—as is all Provence for that matter—and while all the rest of Provence is silver in tone because the earth itself is founded on a chalk basis—which you will see at its best at Les Baux. What an amazing place—for the earth is very red—full of iron—below the unique mountain of Sainte-Victoire, which "en face" looks like a mountain and really isn't, but is the abrupt ending of a granite cliff—no mountain has ever received so much attention as this one from Cézanne. He did it at all angles in all lights and the extension of its form into space forms the unique design of so many of Cézanne's remarkable pictures.

Probably one of the best studies of the Cézanne motive and his treatment of it was made by Erle Loran of Minneapolis—a painter then religiously imbued with all of Cézanne's ideas—who made a photo of every approachable motive of Cézanne and reproduced the Cézanne study of it, which appeared in the "Arts" magazine.[99] This study shows in an estimable degree just how true Cézanne was to his nature—and how he understood the laws of each composition—producing the true rhythmic sensation of all of this highly original scene in nature.

The long struggle of Cézanne had its reward—for he did "produce an apple that would astonish Paris," and the rest is legend.

You might have seen any of these works of art long before that in through the soiled windows of Vollard in the rue Laffitte. Or you could also see little stray studies of Picasso further up at Sagot's. Vollard's windows were never washed—and it took a strong nature to get in there at all—but you could see these things with Gauguins and what all else, often upside down—with a replica of Matisse's bronze slave standing forever in the window.

Having made so much money off Cézanne—having sold a house full of them to Monsieur Pellerin who lived outside of Paris—and whose home you could then visit by card—once in the week on Wednesdays—there was talk that Vollard was to give the rest to the State of France as a

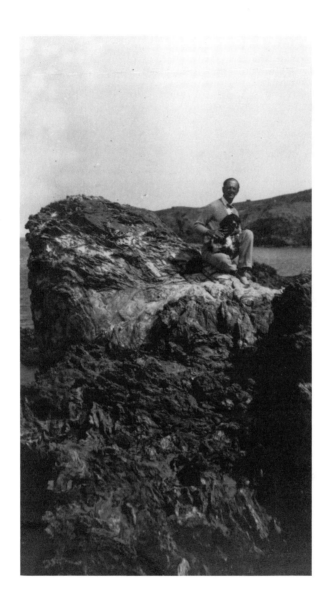

Hartley with his dog in southern France, ca.
1926–27, Marsden Hartley Collection, Yale
Collection of American Literature, Beinecke Rare
Book and Manuscript Library, Yale University.

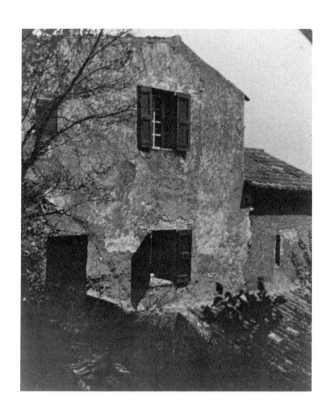

Maison Maria, Aix-en-Provence, ca. 1928–29,
Marsden Hartley Memorial Collection, Museum of
Art, Bates College.

monument. There was also talk that Pellerin was to do the same but the estate seemed to have changed that idea.

There are Cézannes everywhere now of course and many of the best of them are in New York and in Merion, Pennsylvania.

I lived in the home called "Maison Maria" in the forest of the now famous Château Noir—where Cézanne had done some of his very best landscapes—"Maison Maria" being one of the most typical of Cézanne's work of the given period. It is a five room house—very comfortable and the best home I ever had—and I lived most peaceably there with my dog and did a few still lifes that are out in the world.

Three years in this house was another period in the education of an artist. I had free range of the forest—the proprietress being the only other legitimate occupant—and as I was leaving Mme. Tessier, a sculptress, was conjuring up all sorts of ideas to attract the artists and the students to her forest. Terrible visions were being presented of cottages all through the forest—she was anxious to procure for herself some of the esthetic notoriety. Some American had come along with American ideas and was proposing something like forty small houses to be built—some Germans had come and taken rooms in the Château Noir—and it looked a little ominous. But I never have heard if anything came of these expansive ideas—certainly hazardous, for tastes and enthusiasms change too rapidly—and probably few or no one can be caring about the Cézanne influence now since surrealism has shifted to America and all. The new "snob" painters are painting early American surrealism. None of them are thinking of Audubon or Copley.

The Return to New England

I had remembered my own country—never a time that I haven't remembered—never a time that it has been ever more to me than when I have been out of it. I had returned home imbued with the idea that I must go back—and see it all over again or see more of it in another place—having done all I could about North Lovell and the Stoneham Valley. I like to think Paul Rosenfeld meant it when he said, in one of his articles on me—was it in the expansive one in "Vanity Fair"?—called "The New England

Expressionist," where he says, having been up to Lovell, "You see Hartley's all over the hills." [100] That was praise enough—for it needed someone to say that I "had" seen my country and that I was not imagining it. I had seen Mt. Washington so many years from the Lovell side—and as is always the case with mountains, there is always the other side drawing one over—and I had never gone.

Elmer Harden in Paris and his sister Emily, who were from that country, and Beatrice Locker—all old friends—had spoken so often of "Sugar Hill." [101] The name attracted itself to me as being so New England—just as when I hear now of "Smoky Mountains" in Tennessee—that name makes me think it is a place. All names are places just in themselves—just as for years Orizaba and Popocatépetl have been place names.

"Sugar Hill" was the name then—if only that I knew it was the other side of Mt. Washington—and that it was the maple sugar country.

The name of a dear gentleman, a real New England gentleman, Mr. Crapo of New Bedford, who had his farm at Sugar Hill, was given to me by the Hardens—old friends of his. "Write to him and he will assist you all he can." I wrote to Mr. Crapo and received a most kindly reply: "Come and visit me—bring your friend too"—friend being a Polish friend I had known in Paris—who had found his way to America, and who had a car—and we were to start off roughing it.

Arriving duly at Cooley Farm—a wondrously replete establishment with every comfort—Mr. Crapo designated his farm superintendent to take us out next day to look for a place. "It must be just camping," I said. "There must be an old house somewhere, where the roof doesn't leak." A nice old deserted farm was found in the valley—in Franconia—under Sugar Hill proper. One end was in good condition—it had a grand cook stove in it—a real "range"—and the thing was settled and we moved in. It all looked very promising for the summer—and worked itself out plausibly.

I did at least three decent pictures—one now in a private collection of an East Indian engineer living in Pittsburgh, and a second of Kinsman Falls is in the Whitney Museum.

The worst of Sugar Hill and all that was that it was the tourist section—Franconia Notch, and when it wasn't thousands of Fords on the high roads, it was rich mansions and private golf courses—and no matter where you went—you came on one or the other. But I did finally learn what the other side of Mt. Washington was—and that settled that.

Much climbing was done in intervals—Moosilauke, Lafayette, and the lower trails—on the mountains now, instead of log huts and roughness, we find summer cottages—with cretonne curtains at the windows—something not at all to be expected of the Appalachian club interests.

I Get the Fellowship

I returned to Brooklyn where I had lived in the home of the Pinch family whom I had known for years—the Alice Miriam Pinch family, that being the magnetizing influence of the friendship with these adorable girls: one an actress, one a pianist—pupil of Bauer or was it Godowsky, one a journalist, and the youngest a singer—a lot of Irish in them—therefore a lot of fun.[102]

Things were at fag ends again—and Rebecca Strand it was who suggested my applying for the Guggenheim Fellowship. "You can try," said Rebecca, also a dear old friend, "you might get it—maybe not—but try"—and it was given to me.[103]

The question came of where to go—as you must go somewhere out of America. "I have had enough of Europe for now," I said to the secretary Henry Allen Moe—who was most kind and friendly to me. "It doesn't have to be Europe," said Mr. Moe, "There is Mexico." And so it was settled on Mexico.

I had had sufficient success to keep things moving from the last exhibition in the Stieglitz group. I wanted to go back to New England again—and I had seen some rocks twelve years before that, when I was in Gloucester—and Gloucester is one of those places you do want to go back to. I had remembered the rocks and the name of Dogtown—that's a great name—and no one in all the years of Gloucester painting celebrity had ever done anything about Dogtown.

So I returned to Gloucester and took the upper floor of the same house I had lived in twelve years before—so I was all settled for Gloucester and Dogtown. There are always some nice people coming to Gloucester, either new ones or old ones—and so I did not lack for good companionship. I made many studies in Dogtown and as usual—and did as I always have to do about a place—look at it—see it—and think of nothing else.

I found the two available entrances to that strange little forsaken hamlet. No houses left now of that time—the time of pirates, when the people had to take refuge in this uncanny upland at the top of Cape Anne—a place so original in its appearance as not to be duplicated either in New England or anywhere else—the rocks all heaped up there from the glacial period, and the air of being made for no one, for nothing but itself. The great shipping period opened up in the sixties—whaling, traffic to India and all that. The men found new occupations—leaving the wives and children alone—and because of so many dogs came eventually to be called Dogtown, which name is fixed upon it and remains.

One of the descendants of the Babson family that settled in Dogtown is an important resident of Gloucester, and through him the history of Dogtown comes and despite his efforts to make a local natural attraction of this singular place—one seldom sees anyone up there save the blueberry pickers in the late summer and thus—almost no one.

A sense of eeriness pervades all the place therefore and the white shirts of those huge boulders, mostly granite, stand like sentinels guarding nothing but shore—sea gulls fly over it on their way from the marshes to the sea—otherwise the place is forsaken and majestically lonely, as if nature had at last formed one spot where she can live for herself alone.

Painters—or those who go to Gloucester—will never know what to do with it—for they are summer sketch artists and therefore stick to the schoolrooms and produce schoolroom possibilities or, as in most cases, negativities. It takes someone to be obsessed by nature for its own sake— one with a feeling for the austerities and the intellectual aloofness which lost lonesome areas can persist in—all of a piece—even though another kind of piece it is with those vast spaces of New Mexico where nature is given up majestically to her own freedom. No triviality enters such places as these—for the chemistry of the universe is too busy realizing itself—or even as these strange wild places often look—of ending a special story.

Dogtown looks like a cross between Easter Island and Stonehenge—essentially druidic in its appearance—it gives the feeling that any ancient race might turn up at any moment and renew an ageless rite there. Dogtown is therefore not the ground for sketch artists and that is why they never go there—much too eternal looking for the common eye. Albert Ryder should have seen it once—and no other that I can think of—too much power in it for anyone else—there would have been at least one companion piece to his great "Moonlit Cave."

The Fellowship

Having the fellowship of the Guggenheim Foundation and having registered myself as the painter of Dogtown—and I pride myself in this—that after twelve years of ceaseless remembrance, I could go to it and find it quite in its original state—I set going toward Mexico.

But I must remark before leaving that Dogtown is no longer in its original state—one of the days in the early fall when I went up there to make drawings—I heard the tap-tap of steel on stone—and soon found a labourer who proved to be a Scandinavian hewing out letters of some economic mottoes on the subject of labour. I asked him who had commissioned him—and he said—the owner. Hence an intervention of the worst sort it seems to me, the same wild and useless intervention that prompted mountain sized portraits somewhere in Tennessee.[104]

And so—Mexico.

Mexico

Not as nicely [?]—do I think of Mexico as something lived through vividly—for it was a place that devitalized my energies—the one place I always shall think of as wrong for me. A place to think of as a tourist goes places—picks up the obvious, and leaves, having done it.

I am not for the oblique chemistries in human experiences. Mexico is as oblique a place as can be imagined. It is a place where all the colours and the forms are at variance with each other—nothing becomes precise, neither form, design, nor colour. It feels like an everlasting experiment there—and there are reasons, for it was denied the privilege of completing its mystical significance through its own people—the invader stepped in—and made nothing of it but a derangement—for it is not Spain, and it is not Mexico, it is a place all by itself and all for itself—left to come and go on a listless tide. They are still naked, shouting strange calls through miasmic thickets—throwing sharp spears at each other. The Indian hates the Spanish mongrel and the Spanish mongrel pities the Indian—though he to be in fashion thinks he loves him—it being the fashion to admire him because he is all there is to admire.

Look at the speaking stones in the National Museum—and come out to the street—wondering what anything else is.

Why should the pains of the Spanish soul be inflicted upon the Indian one? It is only four years ago they stopped them crawling on their hands and knees three miles out of Mexico City to Guadeloupe—where Mary appeared once to the hyperextatic Indians—and now a church as ugly as it is costly—in the style of Sacre Cœur in Montmartre.

Grandeur of scene, splendour of race—smouldering volcanoes, fine coloured birds—the most amazing light eye has ever encountered, which few Mexicans ever seek—either pure or mestizo—pestilence, miasmas, crocodiles, aigrettes, lizards—flame consuming the whole aspect of life. You feel as if, touching anyone, he would ignite of himself and consume.

No man is important in Mexico—for man is not—he is something to be removed if he obstructs and he is likely to obstruct the purpose of someone. If a man lives out a life—it is usually because he has caused no anger, and no one will bother much about him until he has.

Novel, powerful, dramatic Mexico—full of irrelevant bravadoes—extravagant notions of power—animalistic impulses ruling everything—to hate, to kill, any man's diversion and bothers no one—take what you want, kill whatever stands in the way.

The Indian has few worries—save what the mestizo invents for him—all he wants is a strip of land he can cultivate as his own—feed his flock—and "flock" means all his immediate relatives, no matter how many.

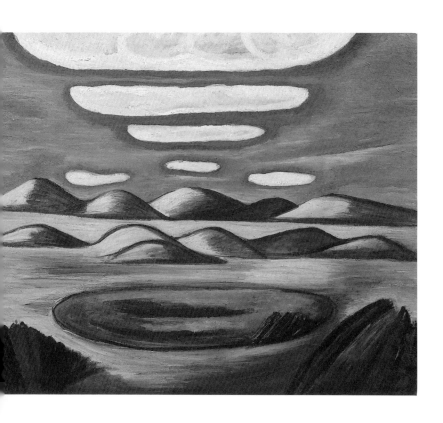

Hartley, *Lost Country—Petrified Sandhills (Mexico)*,
1932, oil on board, private collection, courtesy of
Salander-O'Reilly Galleries.

You will never see hands anywhere smaller or busier than these Indian hands—like a bird claw weaving in and out making endless things of utility and charm—all objects of utility practical as to form, pleasing to the eye—always the touch of the true artist in any little thing, for the Indian is an artist first of all. It came down to him from his great people and was not brought to him by the invader. He has no bed, sleeps in a straw mat of his own weaving, sleeps in his clothes, murmurs softly out of his own beats, eats often what looks like incredible food—heaps and heaps of viscera boiled in fat, grinds his food with perfect teeth—ancient survival of eating hard foods that need grinding. Will an Indian ever need a dentist? Never, probably. He will wash his food down with fiery liquids—beaming in flesh—and spirit.

No wonder the Indian hates the mestizo for he cannot trust the mixtures of blood that flow in him—what conflict, all fighting inside—Negro darkness, Chinese stoicism, Japanese cunning, German solidity, Moorish glamour. The Indian wants to be left alone with his own Mexico—and never will be—for the foreigners pester him with alien ideas.

He is not interested in modern machinery—finds it has no place in Indian concepts. He has his hands, wants to use them—and what he can conjure with his hands he has put his whole nature into—and his being is satisfied. Modernism is for commerce but not for private release.

Someone in the last street fair for promoting home industries invented a machine for cutting tortillas out by the dozen in the manner of the American doughnut machine. It is very slick and talks like a machine—and the tortillas look real but they are not for they have not been slapped into shape by Indian hands—a music that you can hear any day—any hour—in native huts or homes—or in Mexico City—in shops. A social worker—that is an educational leader with the good of the Indian at heart—says it complicates the problem of Indian life tremendously—for the Indian woman spends twelve to fourteen hours a day making tortillas—and if they are made for her mechanically, a racial urge is destroyed and she must be taught how to employ those fourteen hours at something else—and what else for a primitive people?

A certain small town in the interior is piped with water—and the Indian woman is lost—because she has carried pails of water on her head at long distances for centuries. The educator, with the education of universities behind him, has given up the problem and gone into business.

If you complain of lack of life in Mexico—that is life for everyone else but the Indian—and all the other forms of life there are imitations—it is because the mestizo is being or is trying to be international.

There are bull fights to satisfy the Spanish lust for blood—believing it to be dignified ritual. The foreigners all live their foreigners' ways—the mestizos pick and choose from all these ways.

The source of culture behind the Mexican Indian is one of the greatest of all sources—magnificent builders and designers. Like all genuine art, any fragment of it reveals the great purpose behind it. Visit the pyramids of Teotihuacán and the temples within range of Mexico City—the little temple of Xochicalco on the way between Cuernavaca and Tasco, on a high removed hill difficult to get to—but worth all the effort. Note the astonishing jewels recently excavated in the Mitla region—no one has outshone them in workmanship—not the Egyptians or the Persians. All this is Indian—and remains his priceless heritage and to enjoy Mexico you must think of all these archeological splendours, and forget the rest. The Mexican government has at least done one great work in preserving and restoring these timeless wonders.

You will have heard much just these times of the great renaissance of art that is taking place there. You will be led to respect the few spirits who have sat thus on top of the world—trying—hoping to recover the lost greatness. Only the impulse impresses you as Mexican—the temper is Mexican—the cultivation is European by way of cubism and the Italian Renaissance. The infusion is through the efforts of the mestizo.

Rivera prides himself on his four bloods.[105] You will say he knows his Mexico—but the Mexicans will not say it—for they recognize little or nothing of themselves—and the Mexican is not likely to know of Giotto, Michelangelo, and cubism—any more than he can feasibly find time or interest to care for the bringing in of Beethoven and Bach. These have

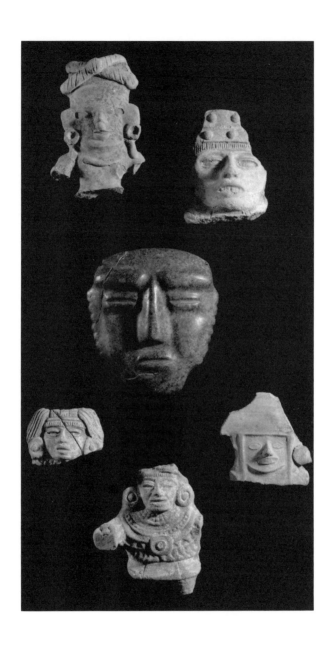

Pre-Columbian head fragments, Marsden Hartley
Memorial Collection, Museum of Art, Bates
College, photo by Melville McLean.

nothing to do with Mexican or Indian emotion—sensation, concept, or meaning—a something, despite the prodigious talent behind it all—leaving you to say, "Where is the real Mexican soul?" The will behind it is mestizo—and you have French cleverness—Spanish darkness—German will to power—and mestizo will to domination.

Nothing Rivera cannot do—and do with immense skill—every wall no matter how extensive is a miniature for him—and it all becomes after you have finished a new phase of theatre with an excellent showman behind it.

There is a deeper nature in Orozco—for there is a greater degree of pure indianism in this man.[106] He is rebellious, he is cruel—bitter—majestic in his deepest thoughts, and touches depths of Blake and Dante in his simple planes—diabolic in his humour—all of this said to be in the true Mexican nature. Revolting satire of a blood curdling nature—then the rise to almost height of height in religious majesty of feeling. All this is in the Escuela Prepartoria—see for yourself—especially those designs on the stairway and the decoration also on the stairway in Sanborn's American restaurant—O so American—that is, O so Californian and Texan.

Orozco is a natural mystic—Rivera is not—Rivera believes in the Russian idea of the People—Orozco believes in the Indian idea of the Indian.

There is a lull now in the renaissance idea in Mexico—and little is happening. The children are still being encouraged to paint in the "aire libre" school where they are not supposed to be taught—only guided. And their moods are terrifying—in the sense that children are not childlike there—no child gets a chance to be—he is a burden bearer as soon as he can walk. He is a communal asset and his labour is but to use at once.

Mérida is one of the very best of their artists in Mexico.[107] But he is Gautemalan of royal ancestry and was educated in Paris—a pupil one time of Modigliani. Mérida will probably not come into his proper own—for there is too much of chambre music in what he does. It is refined, noble, pure, completely devoid of theatricism as he himself is—a gentle, most intelligent, most engaging person. He will not move the Mexicans but they may be happy in having him because his comprehension of art is exact—refined—and he speaks the language of art without auspicion.

Siqueiros is Mexico's best sculptor even though he paints it.[108] He can make a monument out of a head or a hand—or an eye—and there is no wish-wash about him.

The three strongest of these men—Rivera, Orozco, and Siqueiros—went out to conquer North America. Siqueiros was expelled for radical ideas—Rivera was requested to desist because of his—and Orozco was stirring the New Englanders by his radical esthetics.

As for music—it came to this while I was there—a large orchestra capably directed—and at the end the vote of the people for the best composition of the year fell to Ravel's "Bolero."

If, again, you complain of the lack of life in Mexico—the old settlers, chiefly foreign, will tell you—nothing now. It is just after the revolution—nothing like it was in Porfirio Diaz's time—gaiety then—riches—swank—opera. None of that now.

Strange country—Mexico—fascinating if you like Nick Carter notions.[109] Melodrama in big doses affects different people differently. I found it too incessantly picturesque, incessantly handsome human beings—the Indians—not the mestizos—they everything but. The Indian is agile as a lynx—never out of key as regards himself—every move in picture, literally that is, for the camera—expert possessor of time, knows nothing of obligation. There is always a tomorrow—he must have time to "be" before he can be anything in particular.

He will walk forty miles with a crate of heavy pottery on his back—his feet will burn on the hot asphalt all the way—but he will sell none of it before he reaches the markets—for there is romance at the market. He is at the threshold of his education at the market. He will hear stories of illicit love, casual little comedies of murder. He will have eventually an empty crate for the forty miles back home—and maybe two or three pesos in his pocket. If it is not pottery he carries it may be a spine load of gaily coloured birds—or whatever—it will be a load of something and he will go home light—and probably lighted to burning with tequila or pulque.

In the doorways of an evening—and if you want to know what Mexico really is like, see it in the evening, either the country or the city—you will see them in the doorways of their richly coloured houses—down the side streets of Mexico. Eyes burning like coals—standing in a mood or oriental poise and utter stillness, for Indians seldom gesticulate—all that is done by the mestizo—their teeth shining out of the dark doorways if they are smiling—like a piece of the moon coming out of a cloud. Shut the eye to all those daytime aridities, those numberless white eyes that speak of syphilis—pocked cheeks—think of Mexico as a place where the most luminous light imaginable takes all the bad away—and unifies the rest—making all good and agreeable to the eye.

Leave the problem of death to those that love it, and the Mexican loves death—as if death were the only real live thing to encounter. Voices will come like tinklings up out of the dark—the Indian voice is thin and bird-like—and if you like everlasting childlikeness—you will like the Indian—for he goes to his grave, a child. All that darkness which is in the Mexican temper will shine like glowing ashes after the flames have died down—and its smoulder sends up little wisps of leftover smoke around them all.

You will find perfect manners among them all—the best manners to be encountered anywhere in foreign peoples—manners are as [?] to them as beauty is to thousands of them. Mexico is something you will either like or not like—there is no half way about Mexico. You will leave it because it has little to do with you—you will learn to take all there is as you find it—beauty and filth equally—and make no comparisons with the outer world. No one can live through a day there without making some accessions to the condition—the light will wear you down, the air will fatigue, height will oppress, the sense of conflagration will intimidate you if you are so constituted, for it seems like a burning cauldron of passions about to break forth.

Tropics are alike the world over apparently—they burn the fibre out of the tissues. Mexico is a theatre—even the cultivated Mexican says that—it is a melodrama heavily imbued with plot—and the plot to destroy as much and as finally as possible. If the life is tame for the outsider—you take the word of the Mexican himself again—that without strife there is little sense of being. Perhaps you can learn the secret of all this dark living, but you will change your whole being to do it. If you stay—you must pay the penalties—if you can't—there is a train every evening in both directions out—or take your theatre as you find it.[110]

Northward Now

The sense that the ominous aspects of life were over. That was the sense I had on leaving Mexico—something for, indeed everything for the archaeologist—a wondrous revelation of a past truly great culture—with a high spirit behind it all—all this Aztec and Mayan cultivation nipped in the bud for it hadn't quite bloomed by the lust for gold of the Spanish—who were out for all they could get and almost but not quite got it either—so nobody really has Mexico—unless it is the politician.

Mexico is like an enormous antediluvian animal that no one can quite manage the hugeness of—and so they all bite into its flanks and take off what they can get—a dinosaur of all but unwieldy bulk. The parasite quietly gnaws into it and leaves it full of air holes. The Indian wants it for his own—but he can't manage it either because he is a child—and so he sits in the shade or flattens out and goes to sleep.

You may be regaled with the good taste of the best Spanish architecture and you will be amused, if you can be, at the atrocious bad taste of the mestizo. Witness Chapultepec Heights with, in one case, "September Morn" for a huge stained glass window and we suspect a fat *pater di familia* is regaling his lustiness therefrom.

You will be told that the Paseo de la Reforma is "so like the Champs-Elysées" and it certainly is not. Maximilian provides the Louis Phillipe influence and that is called "Old Spanish." Victoria provided snuff boxes and watch fobs. Cubistic architecture is in vogue—quite the best substitute for the modern day because it is extremely well adapted to the air, the light, and the atmosphere—permanent waves, lipsticks—and if a woman is chic, and some of them are—they have either been to Paris or bought local adaptations. There is a strong impetus to modern shorts, good boxing, and a line-up of good swimmers who have to content themselves with pools as there is no water this side of Vera Cruz or Acapulco.

Two of the sublimest volcanoes the earth can boast of—Orizaba—and Popacatéptl—something to see and remember. Great pyramids in the range of both of them—temples strewn here and there on the lava crusts that form the surrounding earth surface. You walk on lava everywhere on the plateaus of course—all the best kind of geologic theatre if you are interested—and a lot of very strange people weaving in and out of it all—the strangest single pattern.

Thirteen million Indians who can do nothing much except be Indian—refuse to learn the Spanish language in many provinces—a cult much in vogue for the preservation of Nahuatl—and three million mestizos with pistols on their hips—waiting for a poor shot. Pistols and guitars: pistols for pleasure, guitars for defense—against the all but awfulness of the gliding day. Earth tremors slanting the pictures on the walls and swinging chandeliers at any moment—earth swaying under you as you walk—windows and doorways that have been sealed up with masonry to half their height because the buildings have quietly sunk into the earth that much. Mexico City, being built on the dry bed of a lake, such holocausts of earth fantasy pervade everywhere—all of which you can't stay with if you are feeling the need of more of earth's stability, and can return willingly to your own symbols of life and nature.

The last swelter at Vera Cruz—no more of the grandiosity of that kind of nature—the look of any sea a comfort really as it is a way out. Acres and miles of water outward—and the sense of one's own North—leaps up now to cool the eyes and the senses. Back to the Anglos and the Aryans who have light in their faces—enough of the dark face and the dark concept—the face that gets darker the longer you look. A ship in the near offing—ready for the outward, the North—northward now.

Faces and bodies whose movements and expressions I know—a nice ship, all set to take one out into the currents of being and existence—into the flow of life one knows and understands. All motherly, she rode away that afternoon in early spring, taking with her numbers who, like me, were craving for their own measures of knowing and being—foreigners—Germans mostly going out of Mexico and Guatemala—back to press feet on native soil and recover the sense of themselves—everybody goes out of Mexico for the same reason.

Soon everything was settled, the comforting look of water all around one—everyone looking about to see who was whom.

The handsome young man whose face had been his fortune—stripped of everything in Mexico but still some of his good looks—leaving him not a little greying at the temples. Going home with a legendary past behind him—two pieces of silver in his pocket and a boat fare presented him by his government—to begin again—real struggles after the incredible dream. And that is that. "I can begin again," he said. It will never be like it was again—"I had it," and now, for whatever else it is—lived like a prince as princes of legend are supposed to have lived—a faded cluster of remnants of rich living peering out of his frayed and worn baggage.

A German baron proud of his eighteen wounds in the late war—showing terrible welts in the flesh of his legs sewn together—every second phrase—"*Tod schlagen.*" Postwar psychology—he will be just "Herr" now in the new regime.

A German bourgeois merchant who had been also stripped of everything after twenty-six years of labour in Mexico—sixty marks in his pocket—stolen from him after the ship left Havana.

Havana, the great revealer of drama at the moment, for the present revolution had just begun—several hundreds of refugees escaping home to Spain, Arabia. Large, portly, dark lady—jingling with diamonds—sharp eye for men—as if she knew or had seen every man on the ship—as if she had "cared" for every one of them—has every air of "madame." Owned a successful cabaret in Havana—much respected by the then government officials—displayed a five-years' residence pass—well thought of among the men with whom she has dealt. The Irish English journalist knows all about her—for he has lived in Havana. She is from Marseilles she says—and certainly speaks the Marseilles patois—the rough polyglot French of Canebière.

You can find her kind anywhere in the afternoon in any of the cafes of Canabière—for she is the type. She is respected in Havana for honesty and square dealing. She is on her way to France to see her young sons who are in school there—such women always keep their children far from that madding crowd.

The Baron is accidentally pressed against by a Negro who is helping load the ship at Havana. "Get out you dirty nigger," he says in English—and "*Tod schlagen*" comes forth once again.

Arabs and Spaniards everywhere—escaping the revolution. We are all in third class—you settle into life as you find it on ships. The little lady is pretty and frail. She is on her way to Germany—leaving husband behind in Mexico—to visit home, friends, and relatives. She does not get home for she dies and is buried at sea—and has probably not heard of insulin. Word comes that she will be buried at sea at five-thirty in the afternoon.[111]

Long pleasant days—no wind, no storms—and everybody settled in for a comfortable voyage.

Eventually Spain comes—fine little ports of Spain—and most everyone disembarking—leaving the ship to the northward ones. The faces of Spain are agreeable because they are all of one kind of thing and nearly of one kind of blood—at least they are Spanish and not mestizo.[112]

The "Night Watch"—and Amsterdam

Amsterdam is the "Night Watch" if you are that kind of person—and you are to have a day in Amsterdam.

It rains and rains. There is a lushness of spring—miles and miles of soft green wet fields, black and white cows grazing, strips of soft hued tulips here and there, carpets of the Orient they seem—spread out to freshen. Bouquets of tulips, roses, narcissi, and fresh spring flowers—every flower measured to exactness, every flower like every other, done up in white papers—and above them pink faces washed with mists and everybody clean.

An excessive sense of solid comfort pours out of all the windows from solid brick houses with polished brass plates—the trim old houses seen in Vermeer and de Hooch.

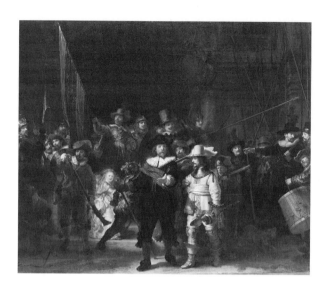

Rembrandt van Rijn, *The Company of Frans Banning Cocq Preparing to March Out*, known as *The Nightwatch*, 1642, Amsterdam, Rijksmuseum, on loan since 1808 from the city of Amsterdam.

Ten o'clock—some real coffee at last and—the "Night Watch." It is in a different place from where you found it last—ten years ago—in a huge room, crowding the room with its stupendous melodiousness. What a tempo of order and well being pouring out of this huge picture—you forget that it is an object of art—it becomes a symbol, single and separate, of all that direct living is meant to be.

Fullest kind of harmonious ringing of well timed—well toned bells— chiming out an incredible hour of peace, plenty, order, system, elegance, restraint—little country—huge heart—well ordered lungs and stomach.

Love. Glory. The stupendous crescendo of all well ordered things calmly chanting satisfaction—surges down out of all this ambered unity. Has picture ever held quite as much of one thing—the idea that life itself is above all human machination? Rembrandt, the glorifier of living essences—eye that senses all things in one, seer of all things in one scheme— life as it essentially is or should be—life knowing no sense of inconstancy—one clear, symphonized declaration of undeniable life—in the continual replenishment of itself. Quality of the day—all things moving and having being—day without end, without beginning.

Earth depicted as completely sensible of its earth meanings—health, sanity—no religion, no philosophy, no superficial esthetic—all that hidden from all save those who understand the huge problem involved of producing so completely unified a picture. Nothing is personal—in Rembrandt—this one of the most gloriously impersonal pictures ever performed—it will take you out of yourself and make you wonder just how much of the "thing" you are capable of representing—passion at its highest—beauty at its fullest—heart and mind at their quietest.

All that music can bring to the mind this picture brings to the eye— pacifying all the rest of one's notions—of one's interpretations. It will cure the "sick soul" for it contains the complete hypnosis of well being in completed degree. It covers you all over with the deep reverberations of nature—as "Big Ben" of London among the bells will do.

No strife, no torment, no torture, no egotism, only the great singing wealth of real being—what a magnificence—pouring out of Holland, from this picture alone.

Hartley's Letters to Gertrude Stein Regarding

The Autobiography of Alice B. Toklas

Partenkirchen
Bayern
Oct 30–33

My dear Gertrude:

I speak at once—this is Marsden calling—out of these magnificent heaps of stones, and you know how a New Englander likes rocks. Shoved myself down here from Mexico where I went on one of those Guggenheim Foundation gifts—a very hard year that was, both intellectually and especially physically—a country so full of bodily danger, I was glad to get out. Now I'm in and I don't hate it quite so much, and as one gets older one doesn't hate anything quite as much and I guess that can be called decent behavior.

But what I come at is this—I hear *avec beaucoup de plaisir* that you have an autobiography out, and I am all so intrigued about it—I don't suppose you run a lending library or anything like that, but I can't tell you how much I would love to see your book and with the dollar sinking—I am so reduced I can't buy anything but barely three meals and a warm room. If, however, you would *lend* a copy—could I beg a first privilege—I hunger so for reading matter and have almost none outside of Plotinus and Santayana and I can't read all that all the time. O how I would so love to see your book, for I know you have entertaining things to say, and you have had a so different life—*could you*—*would you* lend me a copy if I send it back as soon as I have read it. There is no one who can send it to me this side of N.Y. and it would take forever if at all—and everybody I know over there is poor like myself.

I hear and am so touched too that you mention even me, which I think so preciously sweet of you, that with all your rush of people you could remember me. I am so happy in the thought—a friend writes me from N.Y. that you say a few words in my behalf—just too nice of you, but after all maybe you don't quite know it, I have loved you since "first sight" and never forget you and am still one of your loyal devotees both as person and writer. I am out of the world of cheap talk about art these days—and entirely from choice, and you can imagine how much of that there is in N.Y. I'd rather by far hear nothing at all because nothing is a magnificent thing in itself.

I read Mabel's "Lorenzo" of course—and know she has another out[1]—but I found "Lorenzo" a little too much for me as I never have been able to warm to Lawrence in spite of this and that which is fine about him. I think he was a hell of a bore of a person really. But Mabel surprises one in her talent—don't know why one should be, for Mabel too has had a life, but I would care far more for what you have to say—O I wish I could see your book.

I am utterly in the world of nature here and it has saved my life—and my love for mountains never diminishes.

I won't go into details at all, for since I saw you last nothing so remarkable has happened. Things are very hard of course in the U.S. and I sell nothing scarcely, though I have a dealer and am no longer in the Stieglitz group—the departure all friendly enough and understood, but how dear Stieglitz can do nothing much about anything or anyone these days, and his work is really over of course.

Do you ever encounter the Hardens—and are they there?[2] If I were flush I would go down to Paris for a few weeks—but I am fettered completely and can go nowhere until I go home again to N.Y. which I suppose I must do early next year. I heard tragic tales of the Knoblauchs from Henry McBride and it sounded too terrible—lost everything literally he said.[3]

But—about the book—if you *could* lend me a copy—would you? I will understand if you just can't—but there is no one who cares as much as I do about reading it. I am all agog as to what you have to say, naturally.

I send this on, as an old time *bon jour* and hope you could find a moment to say yes or no about the book. I hope you will have a tremendous success with it in the U.S.—you should by all means.

At all events—love and best wishes to you and to Alice T. I never forget you.

Devotedly,
Marsden

American Express Co.
Munich Germany
Bavaria

I am utterly alone here—know no one—but Bavaria is quite another world, and I like so much their abiding love for Ludwig and his blue and white flag.

———————————

November 14, 1933

Dearest Gertrude:

How shall I begin—if I try to run off the words as they first came to me when the maid brought in the package with the breakfast one morning, is it a week ago already, must be, for I have been to Munich since—a book I said by the look of the package and then I saw such a gay flutter of French stamps—good God I said to myself, it is Gertrude sending the book, how can anyone be so kind, and I spilled coffee on the bed puff from excitement and had to wash it out later and dry it at the steam pipes as I don't like to disturb the life of peasants in these ways—I fairly trembled, quivered, shook, gasped, sighed—what did I really do to think that not only you sent it and with such dispatch, but that you gave it all blazing with so much love as I haven't had in script for ages and ages, and how heavenly to have it come to me out of the past and the present and the future, well dearest Gertrude you see I am as high-sterical now as I was when the book came, but I want you to have it just as it affected me when I opened all the wrappers even though you may want to cry for godsake *"Assez"*—be calm—but you can do nothing about it for it is the mountains that make me leap over them to say thank you Miss Toklas for telling me all about Miss Stein and her room.

Well Gertrude that is one way to begin, and another way is this—I started and read like a little boy behind the woodpile when he stole his first Nick Carter from somebody's pocket[4]—alas I am disgusted now that I never read Nick Carter it would have been so good for me then—anyhow I read and I read and I read, and it got lunch time, I washed and dressed for I usually sit around *negligé* until noon when there are bushels of steam heat to make it possible—then I went and ate and went and walked and came home and went to reading again, and read until I had finished it once, and then I began the next day and started it all over again, and as you know if you like a book you can always do that, at least I can because you never get all of what there is when you read thick and fast—and what a welter of lovely things comes up out of this book for me who feel I know every psychic inch of that room, because you will or maybe not be surprised to hear that I have lived a lot in that room since I was out of it. But really what fun, what splendour, and what charm come up out of the book, and it is something that everybody must read and I hear everybody in N.Y. is—and anybody who was ever in that room must certainly have it, and that "I" should have it all for my own, well all I can say is goody-goody Christmas came before its time, and when it does come and someone says did you get any gifts I will say yes I got Gertrude's book for Christmas.

And it is all told so well so directly and so flowingly, as of course it would be and I of course enjoyed the various portraits of those whom I did not know like Marie Laurencin and Apollinaire, of whom I knew only slight things in the outer way. I couldn't help either but titter a little at the portrait of Pound—all right if you happened to be a village—Pound from Kansas or was it Ioway—and I couldn't help but titter again at the Hemingway one—well you did get them all down and it is a very good book indeed—of course I always like books that people write about themselves no matter who they are, and three years ago at Gloucester, Massachusetts, I read the books of Emma Eames, Schumann-Heink, Otis Skinner, and an amazing book by a professional diver—Tom Eadie, called "I like Diving"—all about the hair raising terrors of that business and now I am reading one in German about alpining by a world famous alpinist and all the terrors of that sort of thing—all such books are such fun to me.

And so the "Autobiography of Alice Toklas" is a fine book and I am one who is glad it was written, and it is nice to be one of those who knows almost everyone in the book either personally or from hearsay, or because I have at least seen every one of them except the English crowd and that was of course after I was not there, and if I should ever think of writing a little plain story of my own of course there will have to be a piece about 27 rue de Fleurus for it was and is a very important room in my own quiet life.

I would of course sooner or later have had the book somehow for someone would have sent it me, but I am moved tremendously to think I have it and that I can keep it, and so thank you dearest Gertrude for being so good and so generous for I am sure you can sit if you felt so free and give it out by the hundreds and you are not giving it to everybody like you gave it to me.

Well, now I have tried to say what it did to me to get the book, and I am reading it again all over.

Do be thanked hugely for having sent it to me, because I am exactly like you. I love the English language more than any other and am waiting for a complete Shakespeare to come now so I can really know all those plays properly.

It is all snow here and I am alone with it, and while of course I love snow and it is my first snow in many years, to be all alone with a lot of snow and no people is quite a little to take on, but I shall manage it now until I have to go and that will have to be at the latest in January I guess, for Mr. Roosevelt keeps taking twenty five cents off every little dollar that I get, and he has taken two hundred dollars out of my mouth since last May, and so I won't be able to stay much longer than January, and I sort of want to go home even though I hate N.Y. or think I do—sad part is that almost everybody that means anything to me in the U.S. is in N.Y. and I don't care for that. N.Y. is grand to be in for two months at just the right time, any time from November to February when they have all come back and are fresh and then they all get fagged and bored and lost and you can't tell where anybody is, and so I always hate it—how they all love to be fagged over there, and until they are thoroughly worn out they don't know that they are.

I wish I could slip down through the night to Paris for a spell and see everything and everybody but I am stuck and must sit tight until I can get on boat to go where it will all be different and not easy again.

I send my love to you and Alice Toklas and thank you both for having been so good as to send me the book.

Yours always devotedly,
Marsden

Excerpts from Hartley's Letters to Norma Berger Regarding

"Somehow a Past"[1]

Partenkirchen—
November 13th. 33.

Well Norma—

I came back from Munich last night, and found your letter waiting for me, a very snappy letter it is, . . .

As I read here and there in your letter I see you remark on the kind of painting you would like to have, well I can go you one big one better in that line for I want nothing at all of them—I never hang one on the wall where I live myself and now I would like to fix it so that I didn't see pictures more than twice a year and forget 'em—I am that sick of what they are and what they mean. All you have to do to get like I am is to have tried to make them and heard about them for twenty-five years, and then you will understand. I went to the museum yesterday only because it is in my language and it is well every now and then to give a good eyesweep over a museum just to recall the different ways of speaking the language, and there is never a time when you don't get some new point of view from the old things.

I am feeling that way now about the self portrait of Albert Dürer which is in the Dürer room of the museum in Munich, and I have about decided it is the all around best portrait that has ever been done by anyone at any time, and it is to be remembered that he was living and working in the fifteenth century when they were doing some very smart things, but Dürer seemed to have all that the eye can have, he saw things exactly as they were and knew how to convey that impression. Never have I seen such eyes in a painting, for they seem to roll from side to side as you look into them— most portraits are an image of the outside, but this one is flesh, bone, and mind all in one. I would like to make a painting of a mountain and have it have all that this portrait has. . . .

I decided after reading Gertrude Stein's autobiography that I would also have a past, and am trying to put it down as an exercise in memory, but I have taken the precaution to call it a "Little Past," for I have had only average moments and average experience. I was asked to do this several years ago, when there was a hope that a book was to be done on me with many reproductions—Albert Boni was then in Berlin, whom I have known a long time, and his idea was to get out a series of books on American artists much as they do them so perfectly in Germany and France, and Albert wanted to do one of me, but he found it all so complicated then owing to the inflation of that period, that he couldn't get any fixed prices, and now he won't ever do it, but I might as well do the thing as an exercise, and when I get away from here it will be more difficult, so maybe I can get it done here, and perhaps you can be the one to type it, if you would care to, as you can read my writing and few can. Assuming you would care to of course. Rebecca Strand was a good angel the last time, and did all the typing for the other book that came out, but she is out of that sort of thing now. Anyhow, I am living over what I went through, trying to tell it with simplicity, and maybe it will get done. It will interest someone to read it even if it is only you and maybe a dozen others I could think of.

There has been no trace of drama in my life save the inner one, the spirit piercing through stone walls kind of thing, for I have had to do everything by spirit since my hands would do nothing of themselves. A story of desire, faith, and despair, but I am keeping out the despair as it is not of the heroic variety at all, and besides I feel as if I had been almost too lucky in some ways, for I was accepted at once, and then accepted all along, and the defects all allowed for, but I am up to 1913 now and that is the first Paris episode. . . .

———————————

Partenkirchen
Landhaus Schober
not Schoben
Nov. 27.33.

Well pet niece—

. . . And so you have read Gertrude Stein—well now—of course I know her and all that story so well that it was like living my life over again. I know two thirds of the people in the book either personally or by reputation and knew her story well up to the time she went to England. And of course it could be of interest chiefly to people who know all that art history as I do very thoroughly for there is little or nothing I don't know about the modern movement because I am of it. I am just as glad she said a little only of me—because she gives it a bit hard to some of them like Hemingway, the novelist, whom we all knew well. If I had cared and I couldn't I would be disturbed that she said so little about me—and so much about my German friend whom I took there[2]—but that would be far too small—Gertrude likes to be amused and I amuse no one much unless you perhaps. I get liked for the thing I am and am in no sense a "find" for dinner parties as I never go to them—I was more like one of the family at G's house—even though I didn't eat there very often—and go there at all after a certain period. It's always better to be a pressed flower in a book in people's esteem than a sweet smelling one they throw away. . . .

———————

Partenkirchen
December 5th.1933

Dear Norma:

. . . The sun has come out again at last and is lovely to see again, and I can get out and make some more drawings for later work, so that if it fogs in again and it is likely to, I will have work to go on with. So it goes, yesterday as I say seemed like a gay day, and I want them all to be like that. I seem to manage to be occupied all the time, for I get up mornings and wash and dress and then get at my life story or tentatively to be called at least "Somehow a Past," which is as good a title as any, and have just left Amsterdam and am on the way to Hamburg which was all last April. I have never tried so long a piece of writing before and it has proven rather amusing to me to see how much I could bring up in memory by living it over again. Of course it is chiefly esthetic, for my life offers no excitement at all, having been an otherwise very simple one, and I am not the kind to create drama or thrills of any sort either for myself or anyone else, just a good old stick that anyone can climb a hill with, I fancy. . . .

Alternative Version of the Poem[1]

Somehow a Past—

and the vast procession of innocents, plain
desires
following heel-to-toe with all but mercenary
precision
taking their turn at passing the cathedrals,
the theatres, the circuses, the lighthouses, the
garages and the filling stations, by the river
banks, stopping over bridges to watch the ribbon
streams of dreams flow under,
noting here and there a special hour's reflection
or some gathered substance huddled into shapes
of debris, swirling in the heady current
of the implacable waters, now and then
vestiges of some wellmeaning icarus—defunct
of pretension, falling from the unperturbed
immensities above,
this for all and all for this—some singing
having been done with more than ordinary
frequency, and purity of tone—
sails forever hoisted, pushed by such
companionable winds at times, or—in the throe
of casual storms, shuddering with involved
pressure, and then—the look of eternal
summer at the prow,
the dolphins of implicit faith careening
to the breakings of dawn in, let's say,
mid-June—
and we, our several selves collecting sundry
baggage for the trek to some amazing orient,
how, having been fooled by each of the other
several in one, and by the gatherings outside
assembled, to note the singular caravan in passing,
we the several, with a nightingale sitting on each

finger held upward to the morning and the

scintillant hour,

thinking of ourselves as bird vendors, finding

words, binding them together to fit their incredible

songs,

this, a somehow past, image smitten, to the beating

of perpetual drums.

Excerpts from "Somehow a Past: A Sequence of Memories Not to Be

Called an Autobiography"

I began the original form of "Somehow a Past" with the usual beginning I was born and all that, and something like the thousand words got themselves down on paper, all of which seemed as words plausible but as words related to ideas, a little hectic and automatic.

I used to walk up the valley toward the east—climb up the nearer declivities above the road to Mittenwald—to study the contours of the Alps at this point—and with as much myopic precision as was in my power—proceeded to make many small and rather calligraphic profiles of these promontories and I suppose I am the only American who has ever given the profiles serious attention which for the moment satisfies a certain vanity.

I wanted to follow for example what I have since learned from Leonardo's notes was the right way to express mountains, and that was by getting the contours of these heights in the exact ratio to their immensity, because without these contours there would be no shape at all merely bulk. And mountains are always first known by their relation to the horizon which they decorate, and just here these Bavarian Alps are so truly composed as to have satisfied not only Leonardo but the ancient Chinese masters as well, for every line of the pencil is a right line, and the entire chain in profile seemed the equivalent in line of sound waves or of human voices as registered by perfected instruments.

How it comes about that nature is so often completely right is a mystery we shall never fathom, but since it is so, and artists have taken this cue from her, we learn that the best artists have understood these laws in nature and have never been ashamed to copy them, as art is but an aspect of the truth brought forth by the true expression of emotion. History either general or private, if it were written with the exact sense that nature produces in her outlines, would be very different from what it is—and for that reason so many stories are seldom true ones.

No one, however scientific he might think his memory is, ever quite tells all, because the mind, registering everything, retains the outstanding instances, and many fall into the limbo of forgetfulness. But if a perfect picture is retained of what we really remember then this will somehow suffice to furnish a profile at least of what really happens to one. And so it is this quality that comes out in most private histories—there is seldom more than a calligraphic outline, a profile, a silhouette.

I am inclined to think that everybody's autobiography would be interesting—and it is a pity that thousands of persons who have lived through so much for which no special hero was provided—could, if seen in the light of the hero, bring fascinating pictures to us, because every one is a natural graphist of what he knows solely by what he has come in contact with.

Most autobiographies are poorly written I fancy. But if something has really been lived it will get itself down by the sheer force of its reality. The perfect instance of this is an autobiography called "I Like Diving" written by a professional diver employed by the government—and I think the name was Eadie or simply Edie[1]—at all events Eadie or Edie was sent down to investigate the sunken wreck of a submarine that went down off Provincetown several years ago, and another that sank if I am not mistaken off Cape May.

In reading this book I felt as if I had entered into an amazing aspect of secular geometries—the writing was negative—but the picturing most thrilling. Here was something of a highly special nature because it was dramatic to the last in quality and character and my mind now reverts to the same kind of pictures, when the given diver enters the tragic chambers of the *Squalus* and the *Thetis*, the newest dramas of the submarine variety.[2]

Something then that has been however fully felt and lived is the proper material for an autobiography. . . .

The reverence of a younger person for what one must have lived is pure yet ingratiating fiction as so much more value is given to what may not have been lived at all. But if one is to have an original sense of experience one must invent it oneself, and this leaning toward inventiveness is what makes it what we think it is—or, as we call it—experience.

Nothing was ever made for me—that is of course a presumptuous statement, but I feel not a whit egotistic in this when I say that my life is ninety-nine percent what I made it, since due to the circumstances of early childhood there was no one to tell me what it was.

And so at the age of eight, left alone on the doorstep of the world, I sat me down on the cold stones to learn what it was all about. No fairy stories were ever read to me, no absurd myth-monsters built up, no games, no elementary illusions were affixed. Fortunately for myself, up out of my background somewhere I was privileged to imagine for myself what no one ever taught me. . . .

I was even then preparing subconsciously for what must be called the artist's career because what I saw as the picture was what a thing was, as I have said. So the picturing began early. . . .

I know how much I have missed by not being the actor in life, but I have not failed as the spectator and that is my peculiar heritage. I have seen wonders without end, and my memory has become a kind of coloured film which I can unroll at any moment and see so many if not all of the glories that have covered my eye with envy.

The foundation of all that was to come after was a strong love of flowers, widening later on to the mountains, then the sea—delicacy, strength, moving power, and the death of a white kitten over which my youngest sister and myself cried, and which we buried in a salt box, as that was the way salt came then, in a wooden box perhaps a foot long and six inches square, just as flour and sugar came in barrels and molasses by the gallon in smooth crockery jugs sort of brownish or grayish with always a kind of Chinese calligraph in rich blue on the front side.

The kitten was carried in the salt box to the Franklin pasture which, as I have said elsewhere, provided us with our Africas, Asias, and Labradors of early experience. It was a vast country to us, now proving itself after many years to be quite a small affair, but it is hilly. On the east side of it was a brick yard and on the west side a stream of clean water running, sort of tumbling through a glade where there were trillium, dogtooth violets, jack-in-the-pulpits, and of course white and blue violets, and it was among the latter in a little knoll surrounded by new boxberry leaves that the early symbol was buried. It was in the spring that I used to repair to shady nature, waiting to hear the clanging of the bell of the red brick grammar school which still serves the youth of the city.

There was to be a change—a progression—necessitated by the death of my mother and the breaking up of the home, to the city of Cleveland, Ohio....

I have no means by which I can recall what turned me toward art at that juncture—or by what means I became a pupil in the Cleveland School of Art. Nevertheless this is what happened and my first teacher in the "antique" was a remarkable woman Nina Waldeck who still lives at an advancing age and to whom I am happy to pay tribute whenever I visit my family.

Miss Waldeck was the daughter of strong and honest Germanic people—with a love of music, philosophy, and the general better things, and it was as natural for them to have the classics read and discussed as it is natural now for the young to build most of their education in the movies and the radio. Miss Waldeck had the face of a seer then, and in her advancing age she looks very like a sister of Blake's Job, as her face is powerful with knowledge as are her eyes with the deeper kind of perception. If I pay much tribute to this woman it is because she was to become a much greater factor in the development of my life than I was to recognize at that time, for what she was as in fact in actual experience she would become as a kind of lofty symbol in memory. It was she who was to provide the religious element in my experience by producing the first book I had ever read and I was already in my first twenties. This book was Emerson's "Essays," which copy I was to carry in my pocket for the at least five ensuing years, reading it on all occasions, as a priest reads his Latin breviary on all occasions. It seemed so made for me—circles, friendship, the oversoul, and all that.

This book was more than anything else the holy script by which I was to form my notion of friendship especially—and the same phrases mean as much to me now as they did then—"A new person is an event to me, and hinders me from sleep"—"Am I a friend of my friend's buttons or of his thoughts"—"Every man alone is sincere; with the entrance of the second person, hypocrisy begins"—etc., etc. I have never swerved from these plain, elemental precepts, as living keystones in the arches of experience.

I was to read Emerson then assiduously to the neglect of all else, as I am now inclined to read Thoreau for less circular reasons.

So that from Miss Waldeck I was taught the classical sense both in thought, feeling, and vision—and that alone made her a fine teacher of art.

I was asked eventually if I would like to go to school away from Cleveland—and the small stipend of four hundred fifty dollars the year—was supplied me by one of the trustees of the school.

I was concerned as to whether I should go to Cincinnati and have the advantage of the Duveneck influence[3]—or go to New York and have whatever I found there. And it was instinct that chose New York where the immediate influence was William Merritt Chase, who was after all of the Duveneck school and—as compared to Düsseldorf and Munich blackness—quite a modern. Even still his fish and copper and the inevitable red pepper, with the reflection of the red pepper in the copper, is by no means bad painting. And that was New York in the glamourous era of the Art Students' League and the Chase School—the teachers at the League being Kenyon Cox, Siddons Mowbray, and others, the prize pupils of which in my student era were to be Bryson Burroughs—Luis Mora—and Kenneth Hayes Miller.[4] It fell to my lot to be in the life class of Luis Mora who was daringly Spanish, a flip but superficial draughtsman, and I remember the fine drawings of Miller and Mora on the classroom walls for us embryos to look at and marvel.

I had no instruction from Chase—but I was an assiduous attendant of the famous Saturday mornings when the room would be crowded early with young glamourous ladies, several with doting mothers, and the usual run of frowsy spinsters whose hair was usually at loose ends at the back— and these were always in smocks whereas the elegant pupils came in best clothes and the mammas likewise. Chase was in morning dress—dark coattails and striped trousers, eyeglasses with a long silk ribbon, and the inevitable turquoise ring on a dark tie—this which may be observed in the excellent likeness of him, exactly as he appeared on Saturday mornings, by Sargent.[5]

There was the customary twisting of the moustache—with well-formed fingers gesticulating in sort of Whistlerian modes—fingers trim and tapering—and very much alive in his manner. Probably no one ever talked more glamourously about the privilege of painting than did William Merritt Chase. No one ever made more of a fetish of brushwork than he did, and what he painted I always felt was better done than that by Sargent, whose style had become the thing of the hour and ruined so many possible good painters by imitation.

Chase was not a satirist like Sargent. He was a truth teller in paint, so in the fashion of that day he lost out because Sargent had begun to capture the emotional response of the rich—and to be done by Sargent was the thing—the prices were fabulous and everyone wished to be done by him.

The pictures by Sargent that have impressed me most are those of Ada Rehan and Thomas Wentworth Higginson in which he felt the need of being essentially factual and they are good portraits of that genre. Otherwise, I have never been carried too far in admiration of Sargent and I prefer not to look at the portraits of the Widner family and such like essays in technical bravura—the pictures being large and empty just as the paintings of Sorolla of that same epoch are large and empty, save that Sorolla had a strong sense of Spanish character in all its variations.[6]

I still have respect for Chase even though he was by no means a painter of genius. He was neither Ingres nor Chassériau—and because I was limited in means I moved up to the National Academy where the tuition was ten dollars a year, and if the instructors were not thrilling they were at least orthodox and there were models three times a day. The pupils of that period were Abraham Walkowitz, Maurice Sterne, Ernest David Roth—the noted etcher—Roth and myself becoming close friends, and since I was not a "showman" in life class drawing—at that era—and did not show skill with the "crayon sauce" method used in the French schools, I was not sympathetic to Mr. Edger Ward.[7] And though I was not sympathetic to the anatomy instruction, I very much liked Jonathan Scott Hartley as a person—and because our names were of the same source. He provided me with my first thrill by inviting me to the house of his famous father-in-law George Inness where after lunch I was shown the great studio and all the palettes, as the studio was still sacred after the artist's death—as his memory still is—as of course he put Montclair, New Jersey, on the esthetic map, the art tradition of that city starting with the name of Inness.[8]

Inness was the lucky painter of that epoch since he had acquired a patron in the person of Senator Clark who bought continuously—while the much greater Albert Ryder was living in squalor in West 16th Street, where the Port of New York building now sits, and of whose paintings I have written at length elsewhere.

Instead of returning to Cleveland summers I began the original return to Maine, and in Lewiston I met another singularly different woman painter in the person of Alice Farrar who died eventually of pulmonary struggles. It was she who told me of the colony of artists at North Bridgeton upper ridge, composed of the painters Charles Fox and Curtis Perry of Portland, Maine, both of the wealthier families who became some sort of socialists, adopted sack-cloth clothing, put on humility, and for years maintained a free school in Portland with themselves as instructors.

Fox was doing no painting then, and Perry gave his odd moments to paint box sketches—thin in quality but quite radiant—and to raising butterflies and moths for his special collection, augmenting it with incandescent specimens, from the far southern countries, such as the Morphos—those perhaps largest of all the butterflies with fiery blue wings, and then that other morpho all white with blazing nacreous refractions like seashell, not forgetting a third which had copperous irradiations with wings like the phoenician glass in museums, in which various iridescence was caused by chemical corrosion, later to be mechanically imitated by Tiffany glass.

During that summer a Mrs. Bradstreet appeared and asked me how I liked it with upper ridge. I remember saying I'd like being nearer the mountains and she it was who advised my going to Center Lovell where during the next summer I lived in a cooper shop, later to move in the next summer to a little and [?] cobbler shop at the entrance of the Douglas Volk farm. I didn't even get close to Douglas Volk but it was Mrs. Volk who impressed me—a large heavy woman with maternal energies flowing out of her and every now and then singing quietly in magnificent mezzo-soprano tones which reminded me—and she was like her physically too—of Marguerite Matzenauer whose voice was also magnificent.[9]

The Volks were all for the restoration of New England folk arts then and were having wools combed and spun for them, Mrs. Volk dying the wools herself and weaving them on old-fashioned looms into pillow cover lengths with applied Indian designs on them. Nothing much came of this however.

I eventually moved up to North Lovell at the head of Dam Kezar, now dominated by the atmosphere of jazz and crooning in the person of Rudy Vallee the famous. It was raw living in those times but it was vigorous, the village was twenty-five miles one way to Norway—and fifteen the other to Fryeburg and, something perhaps difficult to believe, you rode in from Fryeburg in a real Buffalo Bill coach and four, and you sat wherever you could on bags of grain perhaps—or much more rarely a seat—as everything went by this one stage, one trip a day.

And if there is a finer view anywhere in this country I should like to see it, for the village of Lovell sits along a high road looking down over Kezar Lake, which is a long narrow lake nine miles long. From the other shore the deeply wooded land rises until from Maine it becomes New Hampshire and you have a completely clear view of the Presidential Range, with Mt. Washington in snow as late as September, and then it begins to be cold up there again and over night its winter whiteness appears. I know of no handsomer scene than when the leaves have fallen and purple October has covered the land like a long stream of smoke. The clouds pile up in sort of large oyster shell shapes—banked solidly one against the other—the sun breaking through, covering the lower slope with long rifts of light of a lighter purplish hue suffused with pale ochre. When the sun strikes the whiteness of the high peak and the lake is black as midnight blue ink, it all seems like a fine example of old tarnished Spanish lustre, which I never did get to paint but always wished to do so.

I have never been back to that really great scene and now despite my gift for objectivity I still see certain people I would not find for they are out among other hills. I would find chiefest of all beloved Wesley Adams, who was to the Stoneham Valley where I lived what Jack Bidwell was to Twinning above Taos, New Mexico. Wesley was a trapper—or to village folks of there, a loafer—and because he wasn't strong in their way he was called large and shiftless. To them he was nothing in July, but to himself he was alive with wild beauty and seemed to smell of coon and fox and bear as he walked, he was sort of pungent with savage aromas.

I used to walk over to Wesley's every evening through the black wood road, with my oil lantern to give me a sense of where—spooky as a shaft of death at one's heels so dark everywhere it was, with only the gravel of the road shining in the lantern light over which my feet were going. Now and then something would fly overhead or at either side of the road the crackle of twigs could be heard.

Wesley lived in a drab little hut of two rooms, a kitchen stove, a couple of chairs and a cluster of objects which blackened as you fixed the shine of the kerosene lamp on everything.

Wesley was raw-boned—tall, quiet, sweet, and patiently enduring—and when I asked him at first whose pink apron and straw hat that was hanging in the back of the front door, he replied, "Annie's—she's been gone ten years and I can't take 'em down because every now and then I think I hear her say—'where's my hat and apron, Wes,' so I jes' leave 'em there." Wesley was beautiful inside as a freshly opened flower; outside in a raw way he was handsome and his whole being was pleasant to me as a shady tree to sit under looking out at a fine view of everything.

After two summers of living up that way I got to know the country pretty much like a naturalist and was not too stupid in the presence of Mr. Sloane Kennedy, the last echo of the Thoreau influence and a friend of Frank Sanborn, the very last of the Concord group.[10]

Kennedy lived a Thorean life in a log hut of his own building on the other side of the lake, and if privacy was more important than anything else then he had it, for he had none of the georgeous view—as he was living directly under it. But he could hear the loon snigger, the fox whine, the fawn bleat, the squirrel scold, and against all that he could hear the soft madrigals of the Wilson thrush during dusk, and these were his people.

It took me four years to develop a sense of how to go about painting those hills and my release came in the form of a coloured print out of "Jugend" of Segantini's "Ploughing in the Engadine," which proved to me that this painter understood the character and the meaning of the mountains.[11] Living as he did so close to his Alps in the Engadine up Sils-Maria way, he had invented a new type of impressionistic brush coupled with a graphic application, so that his pictures were peculiarly "life-like" regardless even of a certain mysticism that invested them—for it was the age of *"les symbolistes."*

It seemed I got to work then after seeing this coloured print and produced a flood of canvases quite large with a direct sense of the topography of the scene which I had studied intimately—sufficiently well for a New York art critic of a later time to say, after he had gone through that country, "there are Hartley's all over the hills"—which compliment I never deserved myself, for an audience is always at first one person.[12]

It must have been around 1909 I went to Boston. I had ended a brief stage career as a spear-carrier, then as specially appointed "extra" of which there were six to eight to do pantomine in front of a [?] filled in from the [?] of the various tours for the second act of "Monna Vanna," with Bertha Kalich in the name part, meaning her debut in English, and with Henry Kolker—Harry Stanford in the male roles.[13] That was in 1908 when the tour ended in Boston and I stayed there over the summer, then went to Lewiston to attempt to teach art in my native town—which was not successful—but I produced there several canvases of an impressionistic nature from memory. With these I went to Eliot, Maine, at the suggestion of the late Thomas Bird Mosher, the publisher of Portland, Maine, where I met one of the boats plying between New York and Portland—which alas no longer are in service else those of us who like boats could enjoy the coastal run from Portland up to Eastport and Lubec, stopping at all the Maine ports such as Belfast and Castine, which is across the river from where I write this, and ten miles covering the whole picture. As I look out of the window I see the sardine factory over at Castine across the Bagaduce River, abandoned because the business went flat as it now is up Castine-Lubec way, and because the country has let Scandinavian and Portuguese sardines dominate the market to the ruination of the native trade. They produce a very good common service sardine at Eastport of which I have never found even in New England chain stores.

It was Mosher who eventually introduced me to Horace Traubell, private secretary and friend of Walt Whitman, from whom I was every now and then to hear nice touches of the daily life of Whitman. The year previous to that I now recall, when Kalich was doing "Monna Vanna" in Philadelphia, I went over to Camden and did a small study of the Whitman house in Mickle Street which was used by Mitchell Kennerley in a frontispiece of a book on Whitman—the story of a woman who knew him—and which portrait is now in the possession of Jo Davidson the sculptor, so he told me when I met him not so long ago.[14]

It was Mosher to whom I appealed for advice in the early summer of 1909 as to where to find a job, he directing me to the Congress of Religions at Eliot, Maine, on the Piscataqua River, operated by an extatic religionist in the person of one Sara Farmer, a frail wisp of a woman who was all fire in spirit and a bundle of energy to carry it through with. It was the summer residence also of Mrs. Ole Bull, wife of the famous violinist who lived in the winter in Cambridge, Massachusetts, among the professors' families.[15] And being of yogi persuasion—also a frail woman—and being rich, she entertained considerably, and had as her regular guests swamies Abedmanda and Vivekananda, and also sister Nivedita [?], I believe.

It was there that I met Blanche Yurka for the first time, who then was singing and had a rich mezzo voice, and sometimes I think it a pity that Blanche gave up singing, but she did become an actress of immense force.[16] My first exhibition was held in the house of Mrs. Ole Bull. The walls were of fine panelled wood throughout the house—lightly stained with grey—so that the room had a soft, cooling, restful effect. There was little furniture outside of a grand piano—and with the ninety dollars resulting from the show I went on the advice of Helen Campbell who wrote some sort of commercial stories and was a friend of the formidable Charlotte Perkins Stetson Gilman, a tall spinsterish woman among the first to fight for woman's suffrage, and was to end her career with a written defense of taking one's own life when disaster overtakes one—hers being cancer—after which dictum she piously performed the act.

The esthetic plot begins to thicken here for I somehow heard of the Rowland Gallery in Boston—long since out of existence—but which attracted by several large pictures an interesting patron in the person of the now deceased Desmond Fitzgerald, a retired engineer—either civil or military—who collected French impressionists when they were distinctly "fauve" and for Boston at that time—well—"simply mad."

Mr. Fitzgerald had discovered Dodge McKnight, the famous watercolorist, who was as daring as Winslow Homer was direct and sober—because McKnight painted breaking sunlight in winter—a perfect deluge of orange violet blue and vermillion. It was Mr. Fitzgerald who became McKnight's first patron and bought regularly as many as he wanted each year, and kept these water colours in wooden folios on wheels which he could push out of the way under couches or wherever.

I was asked to come and meet Mr. Fitzgerald at Rowland's and then he took me out to see his Monets, Sisleys, and whatevers, though I recall no Renoirs at all as landscape seemed to be this gentleman's hobby.

His office was in his house at the end of the main hall. It was a smallish room but it was covered from head to foot with Boudins, perhaps the loveliest of all marine painters and whose bristling little port scenes I still admire.[17]

I had put the price of $200 on the three canvases and afterward visited McKnight down at Sandwich, Cape Cod, with Mr. Fitzgerald. I remember Mrs. McKnight was a French woman and the lunch was as French as anything could be. We returned to Boston and a day or so later I was asked to return to Mr. Fitzgerald's house with the idea of meeting the great John Sargent.

I don't know why this didn't seem to thrill me much, but the meeting did not take place—and perhaps was he at the beck and call of Mrs. Isabella Gardner at the time? At all events Mr. Fitzgerald sat down at his desk among the lovely little lively Boudins and wrote out a check for $400. So I thanked him and said, "Please choose whichever two you want," and he said, "I'll take that one if it's all right with you."

With that vast sum I rushed back to the Stoneham Valley and began the series of mountain pictures under the pressure of Segantini's influence which later were to bring me to the surface as a new esthetic adventurer.

I remember meeting Maurice and Charles Prendergast that winter.[18] They were living on Mt. Vernon Street in Boston—Maurice painting his tapestrylike pictures, Charles making a high grade sort of frame. Maurice was nearly stone deaf but very lovable, and if there was a flaming enthusiast, it was Maurice, for whatever he liked. He was one of the first to like Cézanne in this country and he was the first artist in this country to speak enthusiastically of me, writing down to Glackens and Arthur B. Davies that I was on my way to New York.[19]

I reached New York eventually and presented myself to the kindly and most sympathetic Tom [sic] Glackens who then had a studio on Washington Square South. He was very cordial and asked me where the pictures were. "At the American Express," I said. "You can bring them here if you like—I have plenty of room," proving this by the sweep of his hand over the place, for he had the entire first floor.

This duly accomplished, Davies came down and Ernest Lawson also. I could see that Davies was interested through I never knew what Lawson thought. After consideration of the pictures Davies invited me to go on an errand with him and the errand proved to be to Macklin Newcomb frames. Davies showed me several patterns and asked me what I thought of them, making me a present of four large frames made of the good moulds I had selected.

The next telling episode was the meeting of some young poets of the era among which were Shaemas O'Sheel and Ralph Roeder.[20] It was O'Sheel who said, "Do you know Alfred Stieglitz—let's go and see him—he might be interested." So we went to what had already become in the photo scene and was later to become still more famous, the now historic "291"—Fifth Avenue. It was on the upper floor of a brownstone house with a longish iron staircase leading up from the street, and on the lower step one saw a small glass case with a gold disc above it, and above that the words, "Photo-Secession," which meant nothing to me then, but was in the following year to introduce me to the best photography of the time, namely, that of Alfred Stieglitz. And after twenty-seven years I still believe his to be the best photography that has ever been done though Paul Strand has produced a close second, and it would depend upon your own private emotion as to whom you consider the blue ribbon man, for each has done photos to my mind that have never been rivalled by anyone and that's going far these days. Both of these men have kept the thing straight—nothing phoney about either of them.

Well there in the show case below you saw the remarkable but theatric photos of Shaw, Duse, Maeterlinck, and J. P. Morgan, whose nose had been magnificently modified and for which five hundred dollars were paid for the single photograph.

However, we went up in the little dinky elevator run by a West Indian—Hodge by name—who was to endear himself to all of us later on—and entered the small dark-brownish room with a shelf around the walls, a sort of model stand affair in the center of the room, and a huge brass bowl in the center, though what the brass bowl had to do with things I never did learn. There was the man I was to meet and who was a figure in my life over a long period and to the present moment in a strictly human way.

He is of medium height with a shock of whitish grey hair enveloping his head. Never without glasses, a kind of nervous, half rag–half homespun sort of person with a "sturm und drang" look in his eye and great absorption in the sober things of life. But with all that, I was later to learn, came a lovely sense of humour leaning slightly toward the sardonic, a flair for horse racing, a flair for billiards, an immense flair for music, a flair for good literature—and he was the inventor of modern photography.

The contact with Stieglitz was easy, quiet, and hospitable. O'Sheel spoke of the pictures. Stieglitz said, "If you would care to bring them here we will look at them, though I don't pretend to know much about painting."

The group called the Photo-Secession was made up entirely of photographers, among them the chief professional besides Stieglitz being Edward Steichen, who was then a painter living in Europe, painting pictures that were a cross between Whistler and Franz Stuck if this can be believed—sort of half-whisper half-morbid—in other words, Munich.[21]

Steichen was to affect the "murger [?]" *vie de boheme* sort of outfit, which I would see later on completely emulated by Paul Fort the French poet—that is, the wide brimmed hat, the black cape, the high black stork collar and necktie in [?] sort of thing—the long black silver-headed cane. And this picture was brought to Fifth Avenue and as that was the era when people walked down the avenue—one of the shows would be Steichen on the avenue with usually two tall and remarkable looking ladies, or three. These were oftener than not Grace Rhoades, Marion Beckett, and Mercedes de Cordoba, who was a beauty of Spanish-Jewish origin, very striking looking, slender and tallish, always dressed in black, and the relief was achieved from all this sombreness by long white gloves and a large brooch, with long earrings of ivory. All of this caused some looking, as when it was Mrs. Philip Lydig who was still smarter—wax pale and sick looking in black Persian lamb, and a variety of hats, one of which was a small coachman's variety with "flat roof," and a cockade of little uncurled ostrich feathers at the sides, the kind that goes with the white leather breeches— tight to the leg—and the black boots with prime leather tops.

There would at times be Caruso as well as other celebrities, and lovable J. B. Kerfoot would appear in an ensemble of tweed with shirt and silk velour hat to match. If the suit were tawny, the studs would be amber and the hat brown—and in one case—a suit of purple tweed, purple velour hat, lavender shirt, and of course amethysts to finish off—all very carefully studied and yet not at all bizarre or outré and by no means "morbid" in hue, as with Steichen, whose getup made me think of Beardsley or Rops and that was the era.

Caruso with short but enormous body, sensuous eyes, and very kindly smile, whose mind they said was as on two things and one of 'em was singing. Then comes the famous monkey house episode.[22] Joseph Keiley was a handsome figure in this period—also Paul Haviland—both tall men and picturesque and both as fine as they were good looking.[23] They both practiced photography and that was I think the reason for their frequent presence.

Keiley was the more glamourous of the two because he was dark and fiery looking, with tight curly black hair, of an upper grade Irish family and intensely Roman Catholic. His lips were always a little moist, giving him a kind of panting animal look.

And so it was settled. The pictures were to be put to "291" with the remark, "Come back three or four days and we will know by then what we think." So at the end of the set interval I returned with the verdict that the august gentleman with the crown of white hair didn't know any more then than he did at first, but with the decisive reply, "Would you like a show—you can have one right away."

"I have no money and no frames," I said. "We will take care of the frames" was the answer, and so my, as I learned afterward, much discussed pictures were duly hung and presented to the public.

The discussions took place in the back room which was the headquarters of a nice conservative interior decorator by the name of Stephen Lawrence, who didn't seem to mind at all the overflow around his pot-bellied stove.

John Marin was now and then to be seen around this stove, as were Max Weber, Abraham Walkowitz, and various other persons in the photo-artistic-literary world.[24] At noon the party would repair across the street to the Holland House, which was then one of the best hotels in New York and catered to much the best sort of well to do conservative people who didn't care for the flash of the Waldorf Astoria three blocks up, with its peacock alley with types like Diamond Jim Brady and all the others of that era, very nifty looking men and sort of floradora women being very much attended to. . . .

Excerpts from "Somehow a Past: A Journal of Recollection"

Those treasures made fresh by the dew and colour of life which the dawn restores

to us, this concert of little things that sustains us, and constitutes our

compensation.

—Antoine de Sainte Exupéry, "Wind, Sand and Stars"

Keep in your souls some images of magnificence.

—Robert Edmund Jones,[1] "The Dramatic Imagination"

I must return to relate an episode that was to have far reaching value. The date is confused in my mind, but I had, after the stipend from the rich trustee of the Cleveland School of Art was out, to have access to something lucrative. And so I took to the stage as a means of livelihood as a supernumerary of course—I earning my forty cents a performance at two a day in Proctor's Twenty-Eighth Street and Broadway and 125th Street in what is now called Harlem. I was always successful in non-speaking parts and felt very much at home on the boards, so that to this day the back of the stage can never offer me any surprises since I know the whole layout—and rose as "high" as to be "engaged" by Harrison Fiske, along with two Wellesley College students—to do the pantomime work in the hungry populace scene or "mob" scene in the second act of "Monna Vanna"—featuring Mme. Bertha Kalich in her English debut, an actress of great power who was not to get very far however in the course of the years, and who died a few years ago. The road tour ended in Boston. I was stuck for a job—and eventually decided to try to have an art class and teach painting in my home town of Lewiston.

I spent that winter there without success—two pupils—but painted several pictures that were to get me in touch with the outer world. . . .

———————

I have little or no gift for exactitude of facts—dates may be found wrong, truths turned about. All I can say is that certain things got behind me and pushed me forward, and now that they are behind me, all I can call it is Somehow a Past. . . .

If anything gets told at all it will be to tell this small boy what happened to him after he came down from the three-step stair at Tapley's studio all swell with developing fluid swells—all the things that happened to him as he got bigger and bigger and older and older. In the hours from now as this is being put down he will be fifty-nine years old.[2] And he comes back into his room in New York because there is no place to go and nothing to see.

I remember almost nothing of my actual mother, though I suspect that like most men I was haunted by the image and probably the callings from the void.

I have a photo of myself at the age of eight when my mother died—the same year President Garfield died—taken by Tapley of Lewiston, Maine. I remember the red plush album it was in, and the album had a silver-plated harp on it. I can remember the awful draft that came out of the horse hair parlor when the door was opened for anything—in the winter of course—never sat in winter or summer. I can remember Landseer's "Stag at Bay" and a picture of a big dog that had saved a child from drowning—both of them steel engravings—and I remember also the rosewood square piano, the leg of which I scratched with a pin, and how years afterward I saw that scratch to my child's embarrassment. The album was full of photos done by Tapley—I can see all of us there down to the last and ninth child—myself—also a lot of cousins from Lancashire and Yorkshire.

In the Tapley photo of myself at the age of eight—I am standing on a three-step stair—on the second of the three steps in this photo and there is a soft silken landscape at the back that pushed back and forth on wheels and some were photographed at one side of the scene and some on the other. I am wearing a new suit with roman striped stockings, and there is a sprig of s[?]nia and a geranium leaf in the left buttonhole. I look at this little lad and say—why did you want to do all that I have had to do to be you—how did it start after all, was it the death of the white kitten that you wept for, wrapped carefully and put into a salt-box and taken over to

Franklin pasture and a hole dug in a hummock where violets and boxberries grew in the spring and you put a bunch of violets on the grave when you had covered it up? . . .

I got my beginnings through the Hartleys and the Horburys of Lancashire, Cheshire, and Yorkshire. The last time I was in London I went to the British Museum to look up the family trees and found an embarrassing list of Hartleys all intermingled with O'This and O'That. So I'm always thinking there may be a dash of Irish in me somewhere, which I hope will be proven as I am very fond of the Irish.

There were barristers, army people, and whatnot in the Hartley volumes, but not a trace of the Horbury, a name I myself have never heard before or since. Someone said, "Perhaps if you go to the genealogical society you might find something," so I went over there. It was a dark gloomy place—and a short haggard English woman said, "The fee would be five shillings for non-members—just going over the files." As she didn't bait me with encouragement I decided I wouldn't be frozen to death in my tracks, and with the thought too that it couldn't be worth five shillings— or I could go to Roehdale surely for five shillings, get into the church registers and all that. Anyhow I didn't get the information and I am still going to Roehdale and it is six years since this happened.

The Hartleys and the Horburys—Thomas Hartley and Eliza Horbury—and that's how this thing began. These parents came from Staleybridge, which is very near Manchester, a cotton-mill center, and my father as I knew him was for some time cotton spinner and the rest of the time dreamer. . . .

It's not far either into Yorkshire, where the Brontës made so much literary history—mad, wonderful, beautiful family, and also Richard Rolle, first English mystic, who did all his praying and singing to his Jhesu—in the caves and over the moors of Yorkshire.

I remember even yet those moors, even though I was only eleven, and my father went over on a visit taking me with him, spending most of the time with Martha Marsden, our second mother. Martha was to become a wonderful mate for my father and a dear memory to us all, for besides being "true blue" she had a killing sense of humour and made my father laugh the rest of his time out—which was twenty-five years later—dying at the age of eighty-five.

I can still feel what I now can call the Wuthering Heights-ishness of the moors, even though we went one day for the day in a "wagonette" for a picnic. I had an Aunt Mary whom I never saw—sister of my mother, of whom I am still proud—who became the mother of two very handsome six-foot-two sons who for one reason or another refused to marry. These sons lived to be handsome old men and died with their mothers' name. Whether she knew anything of George Eliot which was her time, or whether she was just a natural radical I cannot say. One of these sons, Charles Horbury, was brought over to Maine by my father. He was a very handsome man indeed, of powerful physique, fine red hair and beard, very commanding appearance and commanding behaviour. I have never learned how he became interested in the theater, but as long as I knew him he was lessee, then owner, of the one theater in Lewiston, Maine, and was responsible for theatrical history at that time for he brought all the early great acting forces to the place—Booth, Barrett, McCullough, Modjeska, Janauchek, Joe Jefferson, possibly Mary Anderson.[3] This town was then of course a one-night stand, as it probably is today if it draws "theatricals." With the entrance of the Frohman circuit into Maine a new theatre was built and "Music Hall" lost its prestige, but by then this cousin had made his fortune, retired, lived on his decent income, travelled every winter to Egypt or the West Indies, sometimes to England, and as old age came upon him, settled down in his spacious home—and eventually died at the age of seventy-five.

That is all I know of the Horbury family at this writing, save that my mother was a forceful person, intensely maternal—mothered her own nine and everybody else's nine or whatever—a general neighborhood mother. I, the last of a long line in both directions—*infant pathetique* I should gather, last of a long line of sturdy simple people.

I have as I have said no memories of my mother save a photograph which tells me she had tender eyes, large mouth—strong character appearance—with her hair braided and coiled about her head, one curl hanging down over her shoulder and the look of much maternal travail. I see her most faintly in her last illness, sitting in a chair for she could not lie down. I hear no voice and have no memory of her words. I remember nothing of her death and burial—I seem to recall the day had something to do with Garfield's inauguration, or, with his death. . . .

Drawn from previous chronologies by Barbara Haskell in *Marsden Hartley* (New York: Whitney Museum, 1980), and Gail Scott, *Marsden Hartley* (New York: Abbeville Press, 1988).

1877   Edmund Hartley born on 4 January to Thomas and Eliza Jane Hartley of Lewiston, Maine, formerly of Stalybridge, England.

1885   Hartley's mother dies on 4 March in Lewiston. The youngest daughters are sent to stay with the oldest in Cleveland, Ohio. Edmund stays in Auburn, Maine, across the Androscoggin River from Lewiston, with another sister, Elizabeth.

1889   Father marries Martha Marsden of Stalybridge and the couple moves to Cleveland, leaving Edmund in Auburn.

1892   Leaves school to work in a Lewiston shoe factory.

1893   Joins family in Cleveland and works in a marble quarry office.

1896   Takes art classes from John Semon, a Cleveland painter.

1898   Takes a painting trip with Semon and loses his quarry job. Takes a summer outdoor art class with Cullen Yates, another Cleveland painter. Enters the Cleveland School of Art in the fall.

1899   Cleveland School of Art trustee Ann Walworth grants him $450 per year for five years' study of art. Hartley moves to New York City and studies in the school run by William Merritt Chase.

1900   Summer in Lewiston; fall art studies in New York at the National Academy of Design (1900–1903).

1901   Summer at North Bridgeton, Maine, in a utopian camp run by
            Portland painters Charles Fox and Curtis Perry.

1902–03   Summers in Center Lovell, Maine.

1904   Summer in North Lovell, ME. Finished with Walworth grant
            and academy classes, takes a job as a extra with Procter's Theater
            Company in New York (through 1906).

1906   Takes stepmother's surname, Marsden, as his middle name. Fall:
            moves to Lewiston to teach painting classes.

1907   Summer in Green Acre, a spiritualist camp in Eliot, Maine. First
            exhibition of paintings at the Eliot home of Mrs. Ole Bull.
            Moves to Boston.

1908   Changes his name to Marsden Hartley. Does series of self-por-
            trait drawings. Fall and winter: painting in North Lovell, Maine.

1909   Spring: shows work to Boston painters Maurice and Charles
            Prendergast, who write letters to William Glackens in New
            York. Hartley takes paintings to New York where Glackens
            shows them to the group, The Eight. April: Hartley meets Al-
            fred Stieglitz and has one-man exhibition at 291 in May. Meets
            N. E. Montross and sees the work of Albert Pinkham Ryder.
            Montross grants Hartley $4 week for two years. Fall: Lewiston.

1910   Hartley a member of Stieglitz's circle in New York, and paints
            in North Lovell in the summer.

1911   January: hospitalized in New York with scarlet fever. Spring:
            visits Baltimore. Summer: North Lovell. Fall: New York City.

1912   February: second one-man at 291. April: arrives in Paris. June: moves into Lee Simonson's studio at 18 Moulin de Beurre. Meets Gertrude Stein. Becomes a frequent visitor at 27 rue de Fleurus. August: introduced to the work of Wassily Kandinsky and *Der Blaue Reiter.* November: visits London, British Museum.

1913   January: leaves for Berlin for three weeks, then Munich where he meets Kandinsky; back to Paris. April: leaves Paris for Berlin again, this time by way of Sindelsdorf and a visit to Franz and Maria Marc, then Munich. In Berlin May through November, when he sails for New York.

1914   January: exhibits Berlin paintings at 291. February: Buffalo, New York. March/April: returns to Berlin via London and Paris. On 3 August war declared; on 4 August father dies; on 7 October Karl von Freyburg killed in battle.

1915   May: his stepmother, Martha Marsden dies. October: major one-man exhibition at Münchener Graphik-Verlag, Berlin. December: sails for New York.

1916   Winter–spring: circle of Mabel Dodge in Manhattan, and in February Hartley stays at her Croton-on-Hudson estate. July–October in Provincetown, Massachusetts, guest of John Reed, then shares a house with Charles Demuth. November: New York City. December: Hamilton, Bermuda, with Demuth.

1917   May: returns from Bermuda to Manhattan. Summer: Lewiston, then Ogunquit, Maine. Fall: back to New York, Brooklyn Heights.

1918   June–October: Taos, New Mexico; November: Santa Fe.

1919	February: visits Carl Sprinchorn in La Cañada, California. Meets Robert McAlmon. San Francisco, then Santa Fe. November: New York.
1920	On 4 May appointed first secretary of the Société Anonyme, Inc. Summer: Gloucester, Massachusetts. October: New York.
1921	Auction (jointly with James N. Rosenberg) at Anderson Galleries. July–October: Paris. November: Berlin (through 1923).
1923	Fall: travels to Vienna, then Italy—Florence, Arezzo, then spends Christmas in Rome with Maurice Sterne.
1924	Winter in New York with William Bullitt. Arrangements made for the syndicate that supports Hartley through 1928. Then back to Europe. July: Paris, working in George Biddle's studio.
1925	August (through August 1926): Vence, France.
1926	October: château Canto Grihet in Aix-en-Provence; December: Maison Maria in Château Noir forest.
1927	Paris, Berlin, and Hamburg, back to Aix-en-Provence in May, and Paris in December.
1928	January: New York; March: Chicago, exhibition at the Arts Club; visits Arnold Rönnebeck in Denver and William Bullitt in Conway, New Hampshire. Early August: Georgetown, Maine, with Paul and Rebecca Strand and Gaston and Isabel Lachaise. Late August: Paris (through October 1929).
1929	April: brief visit again to Aix-en-Provence. November: back to Paris, then Hamburg, Berlin, and Dresden.

1930   On 5 March sails for New York. Lives in Brooklyn with sisters of Alice Miriam Pinch. Summer at Sugar Hill near Franconia, New Hampshire. November: New York, Pierrepont Hotel, Brooklyn.

1931   Severely ill with bronchitis. March: receives Guggenheim grant. Summer: Dogtown, Gloucester, Massachusetts. December: spends Christmas in Cleveland with his sisters and their families.

1932   March: Mexico City; May: Cuernavaca; November: Mexico City.

1933   April: leaves from Vera Cruz for Germany with a stop in Amsterdam. Summer: Hamburg. September or October (through February 1934): Garmisch-Partenkirchen.

        November–December: writes "Somehow a Past"

1934   February: New York; summer: Gloucester; fall: New York.

1935   Summer: Bermuda. September: Blue Rocks, Nova Scotia. November–December: lives with Mason family at Eastern Points, Nova Scotia. December: New York.

1936   July: returns to Eastern Points, Nova Scotia. September: Alty and Donny Mason killed at sea. December: New York.

1937   On 20 April last exhibition with Stieglitz at An American Place. Summer: Georgetown, Maine. Fall: Portland, Maine.

1938   Spring: first exhibition at Hudson D. Walker Gallery in New York City. Summer–November: Vinalhaven, Maine. November: Boston.

1939   Winter: New York City; summer: Portland, then stays with John and Clair Evans in West Brookville, Maine; September–December: Bangor, Maine, and visits Mt. Katahdin.

1940   New York City. Summer: Corea, Maine.

1941   Winter in Bangor, Maine. March: Hotel Winslow, New York City. Summer: Corea. December: Cincinnati, and Cleveland and Christmas with his family.

1942   Returns to New York, then to Corea.

1943   January: New York; July: Corea, very ill; dies at Ellsworth, Maine, 2 September.

Introduction: Marsden Hartley: Practicing the "Eyes" in Autobiography

1. Two major early studies in the 1940s and 1950s, though largely unpublished, laid the foundations for later Hartley scholarship: the Elizabeth McCausland papers, now collected by the Archives of American Art, Washington, DC (hereafter AAA), and Robert Northcutt Burlingame's "Marsden Hartley: A Study of His Life and Creative Achievement" (Ph.D. diss., Brown University, 1953), which focuses on Hartley as a writer. Nothing definitive circulated in print, however, until Barbara Haskell's catalog, *Marsden Hartley* (New York: Whitney Museum of American Art, 1980). Since then several important books on Hartley have appeared, including a monograph, Gail Scott's *Marsden Hartley* (New York: Abbeville Press, 1988); Jeanne Hokin's *Pinnacles and Pyramids: The Art of Marsden Hartley* (Albuquerque: University of New Mexico Press, 1993), which focuses on Hartley's persistent exploration of the theme of the mountain; and a biography, Townsend Ludington's *Marsden Hartley: The Biography of an American Artist* (Boston: Little, Brown and Company, 1992).

2. Gertrude Stein to Alfred Stieglitz, undated [1913], Yale Collection of American Literature, Beinecke Rare Book and Manuscript Library (hereafter YCAL).

3. The archetype was codified by Rudolf and Margot Wittkower in *Born Under Saturn: The Character and Conduct of Artists* (New York: W. W. Norton and Co., 1963).

4. Mabel Dodge Luhan, *Movers and Shakers* (New York, Harcourt, Brace and Co., 1936), p. 72.

5. A fourth volume of poetry, *Selected Poems*, was published two years after his death, in 1945, and recently several more volumes of his writings have been published: a collection of essays, *On Art*, ed. Gail Scott (New York: Horizon Press, 1982); a prose-poem, *Cleophas and His Own, A North Atlantic Tragedy*, (Halifax: Nova Scotia College of Art and Design, 1982); and *The Collected Poems of Marsden Hartley, 1904–1943*, ed. Gail Scott (Santa Rosa, CA: Black Sparrow Press, 1987).

6. Other evidence includes (a) the fact that, of the three, SAPI corresponds most closely to the description of the autobiographical writing embodied in Hartley's letters to Norma Berger; and (b) a typescript version of only one of the handwritten manuscripts also exists at Yale—and again it is SAPI. It does not seem to have been typed by Hartley, and very likely was typed by Norma, possibly after Hartley's death. In any event it would seem that this typist (Norma?) privileged the papers identified here as SAPI over the other, mostly later, segments of SAP in Hartley's handwriting.

7. The handwritten form of the version printed with the principal text in this volume is grouped together with the later SAP3 in the Yale collections, but a typed copy of it was at some point made part of the typescript of SAP1 (both arrangements probably made by Norma). The other version, printed here as appendix 3, is taken from an original typescript in Hartley's distinctive typing style, with handwritten corrections made by him.

8. Marsden Hartley to Norma Berger, July 1910, YCAL.

9. As seen, for example, in Scott, ed., *On Art*. Hartley's criticism was avowedly subjective, aimed not at theory, but at articulating a reader's interaction with a work of literature or art. Hartley called them "not criticisms, but rhythmical reactions in words" (letter to Kenneth Hayes Miller, 10 June 1920, as cited in *On Art*, p. 52).

10. Catalog statement, 291, January–February 1914, reprinted in *Camera Work*, no. 45 (January 1914): 16–18.

11. Of course, months before their publication in *Camera Work* in August 1912 (at which time Hartley was already in Europe). Gertrude Stein's nondescriptive verbal "portraits" of Picasso, Matisse, Mabel Dodge, and others were present at Stieglitz's gallery in manuscript—Hartley would have seen them before he left. He also referred to many of his essays on artists and writers as "portraits."

12. Thanks to George L. Hersey for this comparison. Some nineteenth-century collage is representational (forming overall recognizable images, a point made by Marjorie Perloff in Jeanine Parisier Plottel, ed., *Collage* [New York: New York Literary Forum, 1983], p. 8). But some Victorian homecrafts pieced together scraps and fragments for their own intrinsic meaning—for example, bits of clothing or uniforms perhaps embellished with embroidered signatures or other words, as in keepsake assemblages or "abstract" patchwork quilts.

13. Hartley to Alfred Stieglitz, 2 August 1911, YCAL; Burlingame, "Marsden Hartley," p. 40.

14. Hartley to Alfred Stieglitz, 12 August 1920, YCAL; Burlingame, "Marsden Hartley," pp. 46–47.

15. Marsden Hartley, *Adventures in the Arts: Informal Chapters on Painters, Vaudeville and Poets* (New York: Boni and Liveright, 1921).

16. Hartley to Norma Berger, 13 November 1933, YCAL: see appendix 2. Hartley to Alfred Stieglitz, [28 December 1922], YCAL.

17. Marsden Hartley, "Biographical Note," YCAL.

18. Alfred Stieglitz to Hartley, 26 October 1923, and Alfred Stieglitz to Rebecca Strand, 27 October 1923.

19. Sue Davidson Lowe, *Stieglitz: A Memoir Biography* (New York: Farrar Straus Giroux, 1983), pp. 291–92.

20. Hartley owned the edition of this text translated by E. B. Pusey (London: J. M. Dent, 1907, reprinted 1929). See Marsden Hartley Collection, Ladd Library, Bates College, and also Hokin, *Pinnacles and Pyramids,* p. 132n.18.

21. Hartley to Norma Berger, 5 December 1933, YCAL: see appendix 2.

22. See Hokin, *Pinnacles and Pyramids,* and Gail Levin, *Marsden Hartley in Bavaria* (Clinton, NY: Emerson Gallery, Hamilton College, 1989).

23. Hartley to Norma Berger, 13 November 1933, YCAL. The connection between the Dürer self-portrait and Hartley's mountains is previously noted by Hokin, *Pinnacles and Pyramids,* p. 98, and Levin, *Marsden Hartley in Bavaria,* p. 24.

24. Hartley to Rebecca Strand, [December] 1931, YCAL. The last title is published in translation by Mary Prichard Agnetti.

25. Hartley to Alfred Stieglitz, 21 November 1934, YCAL. Papini does not use the phrase "mystery of opening," but does refer to this event of Augustine's conversion, occasioned by a voice telling him to *open* a volume of the Pauline epistles and read.

26. Hartley to Gertrude Stein, [September–October 1912], YCAL. "Carlock" has never been identified.

27. The best summary of the correspondence is still Donald Gallup's "The Weaving of a Pattern: Marsden Hartley and Gertrude Stein," *Magazine of Art* 41 (November 1948): 256–61.

28. Hartley to Gertrude Stein [June 1913], YCAL.

29. Gertrude Stein to Alfred Stieglitz, undated [1913], YCAL.

30. Hartley to Gertrude Stein, August 1913, YCAL. "IIIIIIIII" was published in 1922 in the collection *Geography and Plays.* The M—N H— speeches from the dialogue furnished the text for the catalog of Hartley's show at 291, reprinted in *Camera Work* (January 1914).

31. The cup could signify Stein as a hostess. It is also a recurrent subject in *Tender Buttons*—a fact that may or may not be related to a more general psychoanalytical association of a cup with female sexuality.

32. Emma Eames, *Some Memories and Reflections* (New York: D. Appleton and Company, 1927); "Ernestine Schumann-Heink" in *When I Was a Girl: The Stories of Five*

Famous Women as Told by Themselves, collected by Helen Ferris (New York: The Macmillan Company, 1930); Otis Skinner, *Footlights and Spotlights: Recollections of My Life on the Stage* (Indianapolis: The Bobbs-Merrill Company, 1924); and Tom Eadie, *I Like Diving: A Professional's Story* (Boston: Houghton Mifflin Company, 1929).

33. Hartley to Norma Berger, 27 November and 5 December 1933.

34. Interview with Gary Gillespie in Boston, Massachusetts, 1 October 1973, from Gillespie, "A Collateral Study of Selected Paintings and Poems from Marsden Hartley's Maine Period" (Ph.D. diss., Ohio University, 1974).

35. For example, Hokin, *Pinnacles and Pyramids,* pp. 2–3, and Scott, ed., *On Art,* p. 24ff. It is one of the legends Hartley creates about himself, ever repeating this undocumentable detail of his life in a way that suggests its epic import. It is omitted from SAP1 but recounted in the earlier "Concerning Fairy Tales and Me," and the later SAP2 (appendix 4).

36. Taken from Ralph Waldo Emerson, *Essays: First and Second Series* (New York: Vintage Books, 1990), p. 201.

37. Ibid.

38. Taken from Scott, ed., *On Art,* pp. 68–69.

39. Gertrude Stein, *The Autobiography of Alice B. Toklas* (New York: Random House, 1933), pp. 12–13.

40. Dorothy Norman, *Alfred Stieglitz, an American Seer* (New York: Random House, 1973), p. 165. This was not the only time in his life that Hartley thought about suicide—there were also occasions in 1910 and 1935.

41. See Burlingame, "Marsden Hartley," p. 261ff.

42. Hartley to Norma Berger, 10 November 1931, YCAL.

43. An alternative interpretation of the phrase, "Prologue to Imaginative Living," which appears in the handwritten manuscript, is that it is not a subtitle but a heading for the first autobiography segment or chapter. However, the typescript table of contents does not corroborate this.

44. In 1936 Hartley kept a journal briefly in Nova Scotia, but this was fairly unique for him as far as we know. See Gail Scott, "Cleophus and His Own, The Making of a Narrative," in *Marsden Hartley and Nova Scotia,* ed. Gerald Ferguson (Halifax: Mount Saint Vincent University Art Gallery, 1987), p. 57.

45. It is interesting too that this was about the same time that he gave up his given name (Edmund) in favor of his stepmother's surname (Marsden).

46. There are some hints that other self-portrait sketches were done at other times.

There are, for example, some photos of bather sketches, with very un-Hartleylike lifeguard physiques, identified as undated self-portrait sketches in the collection of George Platt Lynes, reproduced in the Elizabeth McCausland papers, AAA.

47. See Jonathan Weinberg, *Speaking for Vice: Homosexuality in the Art of Charles Demuth, Marsden Hartley, and the First American Avant-Garde* (New Haven: Yale University Press, 1993), pp. 185–90.

48. It is typical, for example, of sacrificial figures associated with certain calendar deities in Mayan illustrated manuscripts like the Codex Laud, in the Bodleian Library, or the Codex Borgia in the Vatican Library. In a letter to a Mrs. Patterson McCan, 5 September 1932, Hartley wrote that he studied Aztec and Mayan culture intensively for the first two months he was in Mexico, and was "in the museum every day for eight hours." See notes to letter, Elizabeth McCausland papers, AAA.

49. Hartley to Rebecca Strand, [August 1929], YCAL.

50. Jacques Derrida, *Memoirs of the Blind: The Self-Portrait and Other Ruins,* trans. Pascale-Anne Brault and Michael Naas (Chicago: The University of Chicago Press, 1993), p. 57. See also discussion of "I see myself seeing myself" in Jacques Lacan, *The Four Fundamental Concepts of Psychoanalysis,* ed. Jacques-Alain Miller, trans. Alan Sheridan (New York: W. W. Norton and Co., 1981), p. 80ff.

51. For details see Scott, "Cleophas and His Own."

52. The years 1934 and 1935 were troubled and busy ones. Hartley might have picked up the autobiography in these years, but there is no specific evidence of this and no references to these years in the manuscripts.

53. Hartley to Norma Berger, 31 August 1937, YCAL.

54. The latter he submitted to Maxwell Perkins at *Scribner's,* who rejected it; see Burlingame, "Marsden Hartley," p. 103, and Scott, "Cleophas and His Own," p. 59.

55. Haskell, *Marsden Hartley,* pp. 116–17.

56. Published in *Androscoggin* (Portland, ME: Falmouth Publishing House, 1940). The poem is largely about his father and his father's family.

57. On Hartley and Crane, see Burlingame, "Marsden Hartley," pp. 74–76, and Weinberg, *Speaking for Vice,* pp. 163–70.

58. See appendix 5.

59. Editorial precedents include Hartley's own editions of his works published during his lifetime. Since his death, there have been: William Innes Homer's preparation of the letters between Hartley and Horace Traubel, 1906–15, in *Heart's Gate*

(Highlands, NC: The Jargon Society, 1982), and Scott's preparation of selected Hartley critical essays in *On Art*, and her chapter "Cleophas and His Own." Of related interest is Scott's edition, *The Collected Poems of Marsden Hartley.*

60. *On Art,* p. 17.

"Somehow a Past": A Poem by Marsden Hartley

1. This poem does not appear as part of the handwritten version of the 1933 manuscript, but a handwritten version of this poem does appear to have been deposited at Yale by Norma Berger, bundled together with SAP3 (see appendix 5).

Somehow a Past: Prologue to Imaginative Living

1. President Garfield was *inaugurated* on 4 March *1881,* and assassinated and buried the same year. Hartley confused these dates consistently throughout his life, as in the 1923 "Biographical Note," and the later SAP3.

2. Elizabeth Hartley, who lived in Auburn, Maine, adjacent to Lewiston.

3. Hartley probably refers to the following verse from Gilbert and Sullivan's *H.M.S. Pinafore,* which premiered in 1878:

> I will atone.
>> In the meantime farewell!
> And all alone
>> Rejoice in your dungeon cell!

4. The whereabouts of this album are unknown.

5. Franklin pasture in Lewiston is the location of the "white kitten" story, often cited by Hartley's biographers, but omitted from the 1933 version of the autobiography; see appendices 4 and 5.

6. The Bröntes, Richard Rolle, and Francis Thompson were all on Hartley's mind and he was rereading some of this literature—specifically Richard Rolle and a history of the Bröntes—in the years immediately prior to writing "Somehow a Past." See, for example, a letter from Hartley to Mrs. Patterson McCan, 11 October 1932, noted in the Elizabeth McCausland papers, AAA.

7. Francis Thompson (1859–1907), English poet befriended and encouraged by Alice and Wilfrid Maynell; "The Hound of Heaven," Thompson's best-known poem, was first published in 1890.

8. Wallace H. White (1877–1952), U.S. Senator, Maine, 1931–49.

9. Emma Eames (1865–1957), American soprano and in the 1890s and 1900s a star of the New York Metropolitan Opera. See Eames, *Some Memories and Reflections* (New York: D. Appleton and Company, 1927), which Hartley had also read.

10. Frederick Pomeroy (1877–1960) taught at Bates during the following periods: 1899–1901, 1902–26, and 1927–47.

11. Wallace Gould (1882 or 1883–1940), American poet, best known for his volume *Children of the Sun: Rhapsodies on Poems* (Boston: The Cornhill Co., 1917). Although championed by Kreymborg, Gould was never prolific or successful. He traveled south and, although homosexual, married a woman in Farmville, Virginia, and settled there, a recluse. On Gould, see Pollyana Martin Foard, "Wallace Gould: A Critical Study" (senior honors paper, Longwood College, Farmville, VA, 1955).

12. Gould is thought to have been the illegitimate son of the brother of Holman Day (1865–1935), a Maine writer best known for popular tales of folk heroes such as *All-Wool Morrison.* Edgar Guest (1881–1959) was a popular writer of humorous verse and fiction and an editor of the *Detroit Free Press.*

13. Nina Waldeck (1868–1943), Cleveland painter who studied in New York with William Merritt Chase and in Paris at the Académie Julian. There is a handwritten dedication to Nina Waldeck inserted into the handwritten manuscript, SAP3.

14. The two most popular schools for American art students in Paris at that time were the École des Beaux Arts, France's premier state-run art institution, and the smaller and more informal Académie Julian.

15. The rule here demarcates the most significant break in the SAP1 manuscript. The material left out or lost is retold in SAP2 and SAP3 and includes Hartley's student years at the National Academy of Design in New York, his work with Procter's Theater Company in New York, and his experiences in Boston—roughly the years 1900–10. In SAP2 and SAP3 the material is interspersed with internal references to later dates of writing, so it is unlikely that the lost SAP1 material simply migrated to the later manuscripts. See appendices 4 and 5.

Furthermore, the subheading following this break in the manuscript actually may read "More 291"—in any event a word that is difficult to read in Hartley's hand precedes "291."

Hartley also wrote about 291 elsewhere, for example, in two early essays, "What Is 291?" and "Epitaph for Alfred Stieglitz," that appeared in *Camera Work*, no. 47 (July 1914), and no. 48 (October 1916), respectively; see also his "291—and the

Brass Bowl," in Scott, ed., *On Art*. There are also miscellaneous unpublished manuscript fragments on the subject in the Hartley papers, YCAL.

16. 291 was one of several galleries operated by Stieglitz: in 1905 his Little Galleries of the Photo-Secession was organized, renamed in 1908 as 291, and closed in 1917; the Intimate Gallery, 1925–29, was in Room 303 of the Anderson Galleries; An American Place opened in 1929 in suite 1710, 509 Madison Avenue.

17. Marion Beckett was an artist in the gallery about whom little is known; Agnes Ernst (Mrs. Meyer) became interested in the gallery after she interviewed Stieglitz for the *New York Sun;* Mercedes de Cordoba was married to Arthur B. Carles (1882–1952), painter influenced by Matisse, who also showed with Stieglitz. Grace Rhoades was actually painter Katherine Rhoades, and may have been misnamed by Hartley because she, Beckett, and Ernst were referred to in the Stieglitz circle as "the three Graces" (information provided by Sue Davidson Lowe).

18. Sugar magnate Henry Osborne Havemeyer and his wife Louisine (Elder) amassed the premier American collection of late-nineteenth-century French painting as well as quantities of artworks from other nations and periods, which she added to after her husband's death in 1907. Most of it was hung in their house at 1 East 66th Street, New York. At her death in 1929 Mrs. Havemeyer bequeathed a great portion of the collection to the Metropolitan Museum of Art.

19. Lee Simonson (1888–1967) went on to study at Harvard, and became a painter and stage designer as well as an author and critic who contributed to *Atlantic Monthly, Harper's,* and other magazines.

20. The following section, which is not continuously paginated with any other part of the manuscript, is nevertheless clearly marked as an insert to this place by Hartley.

21. N. E. Montross was a New York dealer whose gallery at 550 Fifth Avenue was one of the first to exhibit contemporary European art immediately after the 1913 Armory Show.

22. *Troubadour: An Autobiography* (New York: Boni and Liveright, 1925).

23. Miller's *Portrait of Albert Pinkham Ryder,* oil on canvas, 1913, is in the Phillips Collection, Washington, DC.

24. For Hartley's several essays and one poem on Ryder, see Scott, ed., *On Art*, pp. 301–2.

25. George Fuller (1822–1884), American painter of the romantic school, who showed his portraits and historical canvases in Boston and New York.

26. Jules Pascin (1885–1930), Bulgarian-born School of Paris painter known for his expressionistic paintings of prostitutes and adolescent girls; for Eugene Zak

(1884–1926), portrait painter, see also Hartley, "Eugene Zak," unpublished ms., YCAL; for Helene Bosnanska, Polish artist, see also two unpublished essays by Hartley, "Bosnanska" and "Bosnanska—Polish Patriot," YCAL.

27. Stanton MacDonald-Wright (1890–1973), American painter who, with Morgan Russell (1886–1953), founded the postcubist painting movement called synchronism in Paris, 1913; Guillaume Apollinaire (1880–1918), French avant-garde poet.

28. See also the unpublished essay, "Paris Cafe Terraces," YCAL.

29. Arnold Rönnebeck (1885–1947) was born in Germany and studied sculpture in Paris under Aristide Maillol and Émile-Antoine Bourdelle. Later, he came to the United States in 1923, served as director of the Denver Art Museum from 1926 through 1930, and completed several major commissions in and around the city of Denver. For more information see Diane Price Groff, "Arnold Rönnebeck: An Avant Garde Spirit in the West" (M.A. thesis, University of Denver, 1991), in the Denver Public Library. Alice Miriam is identified in pages following. Charles Demuth (1883–1935) was a well-known American painter.

30. Wilhelm Uhde (1874–1947), dealer and friend of Henri Rousseau (1844–1910), or the Douanier, so-called naive artist whose dreamlike scenes were touted by Picasso, Apollinaire, the surrealist artists, and others.

31. See also Hartley's "Gertrude Stein," unpublished essay, YCAL.

32. Jean de Reszke (1850–1925), Polish-born singing master in New York, also teacher of Emma Eames.

33. Giulio Gatti-Casazza (1869–1940), Italian impresario, was director of La Scala in Milan. In 1908 and with Toscanini, he was engaged by New York's Metropolitan Opera and from 1910 to 1935 served as the longest-tenured general manager in the history of the house. Geraldine Farrar (1882–1967) was a prima donna of the Metropolitan Opera, specializing in the starring roles in *Carmen* and *Madame Butterfly.*

34. "The Snow Maiden," written by Nikolay Rimsky-Korsakov, premiered in Russia in 1882.

35. Robert Delaunay (1885–1941), French painter and founder of the movement called Orphism; Sonja Terk Delaunay (1885–1979), his wife, also an Orphist painter; Samuel Halpert (1884–1930), born in Russia, raised in New Jersey, was a student of Henry McBride. Though a conservative interpreter of fauvist scene painting, Halpert contributed work to the famous American premier of avant-garde and abstract art, the Armory Show, New York, 1913.

36. Reference is to *The Autobiography of Alice B. Toklas* (New York: Random House, 1933): "The Saturday evenings in those early days were frequented by many hungarians ..." (pp. 95–95).

37. Bruce probably refers to Patrick Henry Bruce (1880–1937), an American painter working within cubism.

38. Stein, "IIIIIIIII," *Geography and Plays* (New York: Something Else Press, [1922] 1968), p. 189.

39. The artists around Russian Vasily Kandinsky (1866–1944) in the circle of *Der Blaue Reiter*, mentioned by Hartley, were Paul Klee (1879–1940), Gabriel Münter (1877–1962), Franz Marc (1880–1916) and his wife Maria Franck, Heinrich Campendonk (1889–1957), Marianne Werefkin, and Vladimir von Bechtejeff (1878–?); his list is not exhaustive.

40. Not the last line but about midway in the piece, it actually reads, "The soon estate and established alternately has bright soldiers and peaceable in the rest of the stretch" (Stein, "IIIIIIIII," p. 191).

41. Daniel Henry Kahnweiler (1884–1979), the Parisian dealer associated with the development of cubism—he showed the key canvases of Picasso and Braque from 1908 on.

42. Séraphine (Séraphine Louis, 1864–1934), popular French flower painter discovered by Uhde, who hired her as a housekeeper. Because they were German, both Kahnweiler and Uhde had their art dealerships confiscated by the French government during World War I and their property auctioned at the end of the war.

43. Max Reinhardt (1873–1943), well-known Austrian theater director. Robert Edmund Jones (1887–1954) later published *The Dramatic Imagination* (1941) that Hartley quotes from in SAP3.

44. This is the only reference in Hartley's autobiographical writings to Lieutenant Karl von Freyburg, the subject of the "German Officer" paintings done right after von Freyburg was killed in 1914, and supposedly a romantic interest of Hartley's (Haskell, *Marsden Hartley*, pp. 31–33; Weinberg, *Speaking for Vice*, p. 149ff.). However, later he addressed a "Letter to the Dead" to the young officer, although it reveals little about the specifics of their relationship.

45. Ruheleben: the word means quiet or peaceful life. It was the name of a World War I prison camp located near Berlin. It held mostly British men and boys.

46. Mabel Ganson Evans Dodge Sterne Luhan (1879–1962), society hostess and author. From 1905 through 1912 her quattrocento estate, the Villa Curonia, overlooking the city of Florence, was a destination for European and American artists and intellectuals. Among these was Carl Van Vechten (1880–1964), a music, dance, theater, and literary critic for the *New York Times* and *New York Press*. Bobby Jones is Robert Edmund Jones.

47. Reed, *Insurgent Mexico* (New York: D. Appleton, 1914).

48. Local 502 struck Paterson's silk companies in February 1913. Twenty-five thousand workers, encouraged by the I.W.W., closed down three hundred mills, demanding an eight-hour workday and a wage increase. By May the strike was deadlocked. Dodge, Reed, and Hutchins Hapgood conceived of a plan to create wider support for the strike by holding a pageant in Madison Square Garden, 7 June 1913, directed by Reed and stage set by Robert Edmund Jones. However, the pageant failed to win significant advantage for the cause, and the strikers conceded in July.

49. Andrew Dasburg (1887–1979) was a painter and student of Robert Henri and later a member of Mabel Dodge's circle in Taos; Carl Van Vechten, *Peter Whiffle: His Life and Works* (New York: Alfred A. Knopf, 1922).

50. William Dudley or "Big Bill" Haywood (1869–1928) was a labor organizer for the I.W.W., which was instrumental in the Paterson strike.

51. This was 1915. Vorse (1874–1966) was a socialist writer, contributer to *The Masses*, and summer resident of Provincetown since 1911.

52. Cook (1873–1924) and Glaspell (1882–1948), as well as Floyd Dell (1887–1969), the managing editor of *The Masses*, were all from Davenport, Iowa, where they had formed a radical literary coterie ca. 1906–8.

53. Hutchins Hapgood (1869–1944), radical journalist for the *New York Globe*, and his wife Neith Boyce (1899–1944).

54. Max Eastman (1883–1969), editor and publisher of *Masses*, 1912–17, and *Liberator*, 1918–22. Ida Rauh was already a practicing socialist when she married Eastman in 1911.

55. In 1916 it moved to Greenwich Village where the Provincetown Players continued to produce plays by Cook, Glaspell, Floyd Dell, Louise Bryant, Arthur Kreymborg, and especially O'Neill, whose career was launched there with the production of his *Emperer Jones* in 1921.

56. Cook taught at Iowa State as well as at Stanford University.

57. Susan Glaspell, *The Road to the Temple* (New York: Frederick A. Stokes, 1927).

58. D. H. Lawrence, the subject of Mabel Dodge Luhan's *Lorenzo in Taos* (New York: Alfred A. Knopf, 1932).

59. Hartley, "Red Man Ceremonials: An American Plea for American Esthetics," *Art and Archeology* 9 (January 1920): 7–14.

60. Hartley, *Adventures in the Arts: Informal Chapters of Painters Vaudeville, and Poets* (New York: Boni and Liveright, 1921).

61. Elizabeth, sister of Isadora Duncan and friend of Mabel Dodge, ran dancing schools in Darmstadt, Potsdam, Salzburg, and Munich.

62. The painting Hartley refers to appears to be *El Santo,* actually purchased from the artist in 1919 by an anonymous group as a gift to the Museum of Fine Arts, Museum of New Mexico, Santa Fe.

63. Carl Sprinchorn, a Swedish-American artist (1887–1971) who studied with Robert Henri and showed in New York.

64. Slinkard (1887–1916) was a co-student with Sprinchorn in Henri's New York school. Slinkard painted and showed largely in his native Los Angeles area, but was in New York City when he died.

65. Hartley, "Rex Slinkard; Ranchman and Poet-Painter," *Memorial Exhibition: Rex Slinkard 1887–1918,* exhibition catalog, Los Angeles Museum of History, Science and Art, pp. 6–12; reprinted in *Rex Slinkard 1887–1918: Memorial Exhibition* (New York, M. Knoedler & Co., 1920), pp. 1–2, 7–8. See also Hartley's essay on Slinkard in *Adventures in the Arts.*

66. Paul Rosenfeld (1890–1946) writer, poet, painter, and frequenter of Stieglitz's "round table" at Horn & Hardart ca. 1917–18. Rosenfeld co-edited the book, *America & Alfred Stieglitz: A Collective Portrait* (1934), to which Hartley contributed.

67. See Robert McAlmon on Hartley in *Being Geniuses Together, 1920–1930,* revised by Kay Boyle (New York: Doubleday and Co., 1968).

68. H. D. is Hilda Doolittle, poet, friend of Williams, onetime lover of Ezra Pound, another time of D. H. Lawrence, and later married to Richard Aldington. H. D. was the companion of Bryher (Winifred Ellerman), daughter of a wealthy British shipping industrialist.

69. Maurice Darantière did not balk at obscene language. He also published James Joyce's *Ulysses.* Stein, *The Making of Americans: Being a History of a Family's Progress,* written mostly in 1906–08 but based on a story she had written somewhat earlier, was first published serially in the *Transatlantic Review* in 1924.

70. Mitchell Kennerley (1878–1950) was a publisher of poetry in New York as well as director of the Anderson Galleries. The program was actually a joint auction. Hartley's works shared the rostrum with paintings by a lawyer acquaintance of Kennerley's, James N. Rosenberg.

71. Collector Albert C. Barnes, founder in 1925 of the Barnes Foundation in Merion, Pennsylvania, had earlier been a patron of the Provincetown Players.

72. Ferdinand Howald, a former coal mining magnate, was a successful investor. He left his collection of nearly three hundred works by American avant-garde artists to the Columbus Gallery of Fine Arts.

73. Tsuguharu Foujita (1886–1968) was a Japanese painter living in Paris, where his works were highly popular.

74. Eva Gauthier (1885–1958), Canadian-born mezzo-soprano who specialized in avant-garde vocal works by Stravinsky and others.

75. Hitler's attempted coup against the Weimar Republic took place in Munich on 9 November 1923.

76. Charles Kenneth Scott-Moncrieff, translator of *Le Côté de Guermantes* (or *The Guermantes Way*), 2d volume of Proust's *Remembrance of Things Past* (New York: A. C. Boni, 1933).

77. Salute of the Nationalsozialistische Deutsche Aarbeitspartei (German National Socialist Worker's Party), a.k.a. the Nazis.

78. Giosuè Carducci (1835–1907), Italian poet. The Fiesole plaque is inscribed with verses from Carducci's sonnet "Fiesole," from his *Rime Nuove*—verses that refer to the panoramic view toward Florence one gets from that spot.

79. Eleonora Duse (1858–1924). The Italian actress starred in a play by her lover, Gabriele D'Annunzio, *La Gioconda* (1899), based on the Pygmalion legend.

80. Charles Loeser (1864–1928), connoisseur, was a classmate of Bernard Berenson's at Harvard and later an Italian critic, Renaissance specialist, and consultant for the British Museum.

81. The Florentine collector was Egisto Fabbri.

82. *South Wind*, a novel, was written by Norman Douglas and published by Dodd, Mead, & Co. in 1925.

83. Bernard Berenson (1865–1959), art historian, Italian Renaissance specialist, and author best known for his contributions to connoisseurship.

84. Maurice Sterne (1878–1957), American painter who adapted ideas from Cézanne and Gauguin to primitive subject matter found in Bali, Burma, and Italy. He was married to Mabel Dodge from 1917 to 1922.

85. See also Hartley essays, "Arezzo and Piero," and "Rome and the Ultimate Splendour," both ca. 1923 but compiled between 1928 and 1931 as part of "Varied Patterns," a series of thirty-six essays relating to his European experiences that was never published.

86. Novella refers to the church of Santa Maria Novella.

87. Benozzo Gozzoli's fresco of the *Journey of the Magi* in the chapel of what is now generally called the Palazzo Medici-Riccardi; Filippino Lippi's frescoes of the lives of Sts. Philip and John the Evangelist are in the Strozzi Chapel of Santa Maria Novella.

88. In English, the paintings, *The Death and Burial of Adam, Defeat of Maxentius,* and *Invention and Verification of the Holy Cross,* are in Piero della Francesca's "Legend of the True Cross" cycle in the church of San Francesco.

89. "Orvieto and the Golden Wine," undated, unpublished essay, YCAL.

90. "Arezzo and Piero," undated, unpublished essay, YCAL.

91. George Biddle (1885–1973), painter and childhood friend of President Franklin Roosevelt, Biddle was instrumental in advising Roosevelt in the establishment of the WPA. Biddle's own work tended toward prints, murals, and large canvases of historical themes.

92. William C. Bullitt (1891–1967) worked in the U.S. State Department in the late 1910s and served as ambassador to Russia and to France in the 1930s.

93. Refik, the son of Kuprili Hussein Pasha, was being cared for by the Bullitts alongside their own infant daughter, Anne, whom Hartley doesn't mention. See Will Brownell and Richard N. Billings, *So Close to Greatness: A Biography of William C. Bullitt* (New York: Macmillan, 1987).

94. Elinor Glyn (1864–1943), British writer of popular, slightly scandalous novels, a number of which, among them notably *It* (1927), were made into Hollywood movies. Her then former Paris house was in Boulogne-sur-Seine.

95. Arranged in 1924 among a number of businessmen through Bullitt's friend, William V. Griffin, the agreement was $2000 in exchange for ten paintings per year, for four years. Hartley later had difficulties fulfilling the quota on time. See Burlingame, "Marsden Hartley," pp. 58–59, and Haskell, *Marsden Hartley,* pp. 73–74.

96. Stein's portrait, published in her *Geography and Plays.* Ethel Mars, Maud Squire, Ada Gilmore, and Oliver Chaffee were probably acquaintances. Only Mars and Squire are mentioned in James R. Mellow's *Charmed Circle: Gertrude Stein and Company* (New York: Praeger Publishers, 1974), p. 131.

97. Ambroise Vollard (1867–1939), French dealer who provided Cézanne's principle venue in Paris.

98. François-Marius Granet (1775–1849), French romantic painter from Aix-en-Provence, whose career peaked under Louis Philippe and waned after the Revolution of 1848. He retired to his hometown, to which he donated his studio and collection.

99. Loran's article appeared in *The Arts* (April 1930) and was republished in his book, *Cézanne's Composition: Analysis of His Form with Diagrams and Photographs of His Motifs* (Berkeley: University of California Press, 1943).

100. Paul Rosenfeld, "The Paintings of Marsden Hartley," *Vanity Fair* 18 (August 1922): 47, 84, 94, 96. The exact wording is "To go to New England mountain country in fall-time is to see on every hand Hartley's [sic] strewn up every furry hillside" (p. 84).

101. Elmer and Emily Harden were friends of Gertrude Stein; Beatrice Locker is unknown.

102. Esther Pinch was the actress, Anna the journalist in China, and Margaret followed Alice in the opera. Ruth the pianist, studied with either Harold Bauer (1873–1951) or Leopold Godowsky (1870–1938).

103. Rebecca Salisbury Strand was married to the photographer Paul Strand. Both were close to Stieglitz, but Rebecca was the ardent correspondent and typist and helped both Stieglitz and Hartley with their writings. After Paul Strand's death, she married Oliver B. James.

104. The Tennessee site is unknown. Hartley may have been erroneously referring to the portraits of presidents on Mount Rushmore in South Dakota by American sculptor Gutzon Borglum (1867–1941). Of these, the head of Washington was unveiled in 1927 although the other presidents' portraits (Jefferson, Lincoln, and Roosevelt) were not finished until 1936–39, after Hartley wrote SAPI. Alternatively, Hartley may have been referring to Borglum's earlier, ill-fated, and unfinished project to carve the head of Robert E. Lee into the side of Stone Mountain, near Atlanta.

105. Diego Rivera (1886–1957), the Mexican muralist who studied most extensively in Europe from 1907 to 1921. Rivera completed fresco cycles for the National Palace and the Ministry of Public Education in Mexico City, and in the United States, his works include murals at the Detroit Institute of the Arts, the San Francisco Art Institute, and Rockefeller Center in New York City, where the mural included a portrait of Lenin and was destroyed in 1934. Hartley's mention of Rivera's "four bloods" makes reference to the muralist's expansive statements about his ancestry. In addition to Spanish, Indian (his maternal grandmother was half Indian), Portuguese, and Jewish (his paternal grandmother), Rivera claimed at various times to be also part Dutch, Italian, Russian, Chinese, and Black. See Bertram D. Wolfe, *The Fabulous Life of Diego Rivera* (New York: Stein and Day, 1963), pp. 13–14.

106. José Clemente Orozco (1883–1949) studied art at the Academia San Carlos in Mexico City and worked as a political cartoonist during the Mexican Revolution. His work in America includes murals at Pomona Collage in California, the New School for Social Research, and Dartmouth College in New Hampshire.

107. Carlos Mérida (1891–1984), a Guatemalan artist of Mayan descent, came to Mexico to work and exhibit in a nationalistic manner in 1919, but after two years of study in Europe in the 1920s his style became more conscientiously abstract.

108. David Siqueiros (1898–1974), muralist who studied art in Mexico City at the San Carlo Academy and took an active role in the cultural revolution.

109. Nick Carter mysteries were "dime novel" detective stories that were widely popular in the 1920s. Nick Carter was the common pseudonym for a list of authors, among the earliest including John Russell Coryell, Thomas C. Harbaugh, and Frederick Van Rensselaer Day.

110. Hartley wrote further about Mexico in unpublished essays like "Mexican Vignette" and "The Bleeding Christs of Mexico," both YCAL.

111. The event is the subject of the title poem in Hartley's last book of poetry, *Sea Burial* (Portland, ME: Falmouth Publishing House, 1941).

112. During his stay in Mexico, Hartley heard the news that his friend, American poet Hart Crane (1899–1932) who had been in Mexico at the same time as Hartley and with whom Hartley had spent time there, committed suicide by jumping over the railing of his steamship home. It had a profound effect on Hartley who devoted a major painting (*Eight Bells' Folly, Memorial for Hart Crane*, 1933) and several essays and poems to the event. But it was excluded from the autobiography.

Appendix I: Hartley's Letters to Gertrude Stein Regarding *The Autobiography of Alice B. Toklas*

1. Mabel Dodge Luhan, *Lorenzo in Taos* (New York: Alfred A. Knopf, 1932) and *Intimate Memories*, a four-volume autobiography. Volume I, *Background*, published by Harcourt, Brace and Co., in 1933, was just out when Hartley wrote this letter.

2. Elmer and Emily Harden, the same friends of Stein whom Hartley visited in New Hampshire in 1930.

3. May Bookstaver was a Baltimore friend and romantic interest of Stein's while the latter was a medical student at Johns Hopkins; May later became Mrs. Charles Knoblauch and helped Stein by passing her manuscripts along to publishers in the United States.

4. Nick Carter, as in "Somehow a Past: Prologue to Imaginative Living," note 109 above.

Appendix 2: Excerpts from Hartley's Letters to Norma Berger Regarding "Somehow a Past"

1. The 13 November and 5 December letters are original typescripts, so Hartley must have had access to a typewriter in Bavaria. The 27 November letter, however, is taken from an original, handwritten by Hartley. The excerpts reproduced here do not reflect the complete contents of these letters, which touch upon numerous additional topics unrelated to the autobiography.

2. Arnold Rönnebeck.

Appendix 3: Alternative Version of the Poem

1. Whether this, or the poem of the same title printed at the front of this book, held premier status in Hartley's mind is not known. This page, typed by Hartley himself, is assembled in the Hartley papers, YCAL, with the typescript of SAPI.

Appendix 4: Excerpts from "Somehow a Past: A Sequence of Memories Not to Be Called an Autobiography"

1. Tom Eadie, *I Like Diving: A Professional's Story* (Boston: Houghton Mifflin Company, 1929).

2. The U.S.S. *Squalus* and the H.M.S. *Thetis* were both submarines that sank in 1939 shortly after they were built, just months before World War II began in Europe. Both made headlines, but the *Thetis* was the greater disaster—nearly everyone on board was killed.

3. Frank Duveneck (1848–1919), along with Chase and Henri, was a major American painter and teacher at the end of the nineteenth century. He taught in Munich in the 1870s and in Cincinnati later on. His work combined the styles of Manet, impressionism, and dark "Düsseldorf" realism.

4. Kenyon Cox (1865–1919) and Henry Siddons Mowbray (1858–1928) specialized in academic subjects and architectural murals; Bryson Burroughs (1869–1934) was also an academic mural painter and later curator of painting at the Metropolitan Museum; Francis Luis Mora (1874–1940) was a mural and print artist of historical subjects; and Kenneth Hayes Miller (1876–1952) was the teacher of many American urban realists and members of the Ashcan School.

5. John Singer Sargent (1856–1925). Slightly younger than Duveneck and Chase, Sargent used a lighter palette and was sought after for his elegant subjects and facile brushwork and surfaces.

6. Joaquín Sorolla y Bastica (1863–1923), Spanish painter.

7. Abraham Walkowitz (1880–1965), "artist of Isadora Duncan," and member of Stieglitz's circle at 291; Maurice Sterne, see "Somehow a Past: Prologue to Imaginative Living," note 84 above; Ernest David Roth (Germany, 1879–1964), noted for prints; Ward may be Edger M. Ward the younger (1887–1943), a minor mural painter in New York and New Jersey.

8. Jonathan Scott Hartley (1845–1912), sculptor schooled in Europe, who married the daughter of American landscape painter George Inness (1853–1926). Inness was known for his glowing, atmospheric landscapes and was also a well-known illustrator for magazines like *Scribner's*.

9. Marguerite Matzenauer (1881–1963), Austro-Hungarian soprano and contralto singer of exceptional range, who joined the Metropolitan Opera in 1911.

10. William Sloane Kennedy (1850–1929) was a close friend of Whitman and wrote and edited books on the poet and on Ralph Waldo Emerson, Thoreau's mentor; Franklin Benjamin Sanborn (1831–1917), American journalist, author, and philanthropist, wrote biographies of Thoreau, Ralph Waldo Emerson, and others of the Concord group.

11. Giovanni Segantini (1858–1899), Italian neo-impressionist painter and subject of a special issue of *Jugend* in 1903. Hartley wrote elsewhere on Segantini in an unpublished essay, "On the Subject of the Mountain," YCAL. See also Haskell, *Marsden Hartley*, p. 13.

12. Paul Rosenfeld, as in "Somehow a Past: Prologue to Imaginative Living," note 100 above.

13. Bertha Kalich (1874–1939), popular Austrian-American actress; the romantic tragedy *Monna Vanna* was written by Maurice Maeterlinck in 1902. Henry Kolker (1874–1947) and Henry (Harry) Stanford (1872–1921) were American actors.

14. Elizabeth Leavitt Keller, *Walt Whitman in Mickle Street* (New York: Mitchell Kennerley, 1921).

15. The Norwegian Ole (Bornemann) Bull (1810–1880) was among the most famous violinists of the nineteenth century who spent much of the latter part of his career in the United States. His second wife, Sara Chapman Thorp, an American from Wisconsin, was much younger than he, only fifty-nine in 1909.

16. Blanche Yurka (1887–1974) was a Czechoslovakian-born singer and actress noted for her role as Gina in Ibsen's *Wild Duck*.

17. Eugène Boudin (1824–1898), French seascapist, friend of Claude Monet, and specialist in scenes at Trouville.

18. Maurice (1859–1924) and Charles (1868–1948) Prendergast were both painters, although Maurice is by far better known. He developed a personal style that synthesized impressionism and neo-impressionism, and applied it to popular city scenes and landscapes.

19. William J. Glackens (1870–1938), New York City urban realist and member of The Eight; Arthur B. Davies (1862–1928) was an American symbolist painter and decorative artist in a range of media.

20. Shaemas O'Sheel (1886–1954), Irish American imagist poet; Roeder may have been Ralph L. Roeder (1890–1970), a writer of historical biographies.

21. James Abbott McNeil Whistler (1834–1903), American painter and print-maker in Europe, noted for his aestheticism and dominating personality; Franz von Stuck (1863–1928), German symbolist painter.

22. It was "famous" perhaps only to Hartley. No explanation for this comment has come to light.

23. Joseph Turner Keiley (1869–1914), photographer and friend of Stieglitz and associate editor of *Camera Work*. Paul Haviland (1850–1950), descendant of the French porcelain firm and a photographer in New York.

24. John Marin (1870–1953) was an abstract landscapist and one of Stieglitz's best-known painters. Max Weber (1881–1961), American cubist painter and sculptor in the Stieglitz circle.

Appendix 5: Excerpts from "Somehow a Past: A Journal of Recollection"

1. Hartley drew these quotes as follows: from Sainte Exupéry, *Wind, Sand and Stars*, trans. Lewis Galantière (New York: Harcourt, Brace & World, 1940), p. 46; and Jones, *The Dramatic Imagination: Reflections and Speculations on the Art of the Theatre* (New York: Theatre Arts Books, 1941), p. 30, in which the given quote is attributed to "a modern Irish poet." This is the only "Somehow a Past" manuscript that contains prefatory quotes.

2. Presumably Hartley is writing the day before his birthday (4 January); thus the year of writing is 1936.

3. All stars of the American or English-speaking stage of the period: Edwin Thomas Booth (1833–1893), Lawrence Barrett (1838–1891), John Edward McCullough (1837–1885), Helena Modjeska (1840–1909), Francesca Romana Magdelena Janauchek (1830–1904), Joseph Jefferson (1829–1905), and Mary Anderson (1859–1940).

INDEX

Note: Page numbers in italics represent illustrations.